Seven Questions

Find the Joy of Living the Life God Intended for You to Live

Bobby G. Muse, Jr.

©Copyright 2017

Simple Life Publishing

Published by Simple Life Publishing
Louisville, Kentucky
www.SimpleLifePublishing.com

ISBN-10: 0692964711
ISBN-13: 9780692964712
LCCN: 2017915894
Simple Life Publishing, Louisville, KY

For God so loved the world that he gave his one and only Son, that whoever believes in him shall not perish but have eternal life.

John 3:16

Love the Lord your God with all your heart and with all your soul and with all your mind and with all your strength. The second is this: Love your neighbor as yourself. There is no commandment greater than these.

Mark 12:30-31

Then Jesus came to them and said, "All authority in heaven and on earth has been given to me. Therefore go and make disciples of all nations, baptizing them in the name of the Father and of the Son and of the Holy Spirit, and teaching them to obey everything I have commanded you. And surely I am with you always, to the very end of the age."

Matthew 28:18-20

Acknowledgments

To Jesus Christ my Lord and Savior, who before I even existed, willingly died on a cross to forgive me of my sins. He gives my life direction, purpose, hope, and the promise of eternal life.

To my wife and best friend, Mary, who unselfishly supports me in following my dreams and doing what God created me to do. Thank you for your help reviewing my manuscript drafts and providing editorial support. I cannot imagine my life without you by my side.

To my children Jonathan and Kristen, you have given me countless learning opportunities throughout my life. I love both of you very much.

To Camp NaCoMe in Pleasantville, Tennessee, who made it possible for a young teenage boy in the stillness of the night to find God, and a year later find the girl of his dreams.

Contents

Introduction
Seven Questions

Before we work together to find the joy God specifically intended for you, there is something we need to do first. We need to discuss the two most important things in life. Until you relentlessly pursue these two things, the emptiness you're trying to fill, the happiness and joy you are seeking, the driving purpose you so desperately want in your life will never happen. Your success depends on your commitment to these two things.

First, there is nothing more important in life than your personal relationship with God through the Holy Spirit. Your sustaining happiness – joy – depends on the one-on-one time you spend talking with God. There will be times when God speaks directly to you and gives you clear direction. Cherish these moments and learn everything you can. Other times, you may feel your words are falling on deaf ears. Don't be discouraged. It happens to all of us. It is the result of life's distractions driving a wedge between us and God. In fact, I believe it's a test. It's a test to see if we will remain focused on God or whether we will turn away from Him and seek our own solutions. As you spend more time with God and your relationship with the Holy Spirit grows over time, your earthly distractions will diminish and you will begin to feel His presence, even when you don't think He is listening. As God told Jacob in Genesis 28:15 and as Jesus told His disciples in Matthew 28:20, "*I am with you always.*"

If you don't currently have a relationship with Jesus Christ, I strongly encourage you to go right now to the appendix in the back of this book on "*How To Become A Child of God*" and start one. As soon as possible after praying the Prayer of Salvation, contact a Christ-centered house of worship in your city and tell them about your decision. Get involved with these people. If for whatever reason the church you selected doesn't work out, keep looking until one does. The group of believers you ultimately choose to become a part of will provide an invaluable support system for you as you seek God's plan for your life.

If you are a Christian who over time has diverted your eyes away from the leadership of the Holy Spirit, I pray you will go to a quiet place and get on your knees and re-establish your relationship with God. He is waiting to help you use the unique gifts, abilities, and passions He has given you to live the life He intended for you to live. I pray you will do this now.

Once you have given priority to your relationship with God and the Holy Spirit, the second most important thing in life is understanding what God created you to do. Just like your relationship with God and the Holy Spirit, your overall happiness or joy depends on understanding God's unique plan for your life, your reason for living. I don't believe you can be as happy as God intended for you to be if you are not focused on the unique purpose you were created and designed to accomplish. God knew you before you were even conceived in your mother's womb. (Psalms 139:13-16) He had a plan and purpose for your life before you were even born. He designed you with the gifts, abilities, and passions you need to be successful accomplishing your life's purpose. Real, sustaining joy only comes through embracing your God-given design and pursuing the unique purpose God has given you.

Now I know what some of you are thinking: *What about all the successful people in the world who seem to have found their purpose and used their gifts to help them become very successful without God?* The media tells us every day about movie stars, incredible athletes, and wealthy business people who seem to have made it without the Holy Spirit's direction. You're thinking: B*ased on what you've said so far, how can this be possible? They seem so happy.*

Even the unbeliever is programmed with God-given gifts, abilities, passions, and a purpose at birth. Sometimes – by accident – these people find their God-given gifts and use them to fulfill a purpose of their own choosing. But are they truly happy? Do they have a sustaining joy that can't be quenched? Based on the things we see in these same news stories, I'm not sure they are as happy as they seem. Suicides, excessive drug use, and numerous other clues suggest to us that maybe they are not as happy as they pretend. The real question is: Can you really be completely happy without God in control of your life? I think the answer to this question is no. God is central to our happiness, to our long-term sustainable joy. After all, it was God who defined for each of us what makes us happy.

I've been fortunate throughout my career to work with many people who are very successful. Some of them would be labeled in the top 1 percent of all income earners. They've taken advantage of their God-given gifts and become wildly successful by almost anyone's standard. It has also been my experience that many of these same people are looking for the sustainable happiness and joy we're all looking for, the real satisfaction money can't buy. You might ask: *How can a highly successful person in the 1 percent of all income earners still be searching for happiness?* I think the answer is obvious. Until we build a relationship with God and ask for His direction, our real life's purpose may go undiscovered. Our God-given gifts and purpose may lay dormant or underutilized. The thing or things God has designed within us to make us completely happy are never found. Not until we open up a dialog with God and follow His path for our lives through the leadership of the Holy Spirit will we fully understand the reason for the unique tools He gave each of us and the driving purpose they were intended to fulfill.

There can be no happier place than following God's plan for your life, using the gifts, abilities, and passions God has specifically given you to accomplish the unique purpose He intended for you to complete. In my opinion, contrary to the definition you may find in a dictionary, this is the definition of real joy: walking with God down the path He intended for you to follow!

I pray as you go through this book your relationship with God will deepen, you will recognize the gifts, abilities, and passions programmed into your DNA, and you will start to understand and embrace the unique purpose God intended for your life. If you can accomplish these three things, you will find the sustaining joy only God can provide.

1

Am I Just A Random Occurrence Of The Universe?

It was a muggy August night in southern Tennessee. Although more than 40 years ago, I still remember it like it happened yesterday. It was the third night of a weeklong church camp for high school teenagers. Sitting by a campfire quietly singing old hymns and choruses just before bedtime, I felt empty. I felt alone. A flood of emotions overcame me as I realized I needed God in my life.

Up until this point in my life, I thought you had to be a bad person to need God. I wasn't a bad person. I hadn't broken any laws or gone to jail. Although very popular for my age group in the

1

70s, I didn't smoke, drink, or use illegal drugs. I didn't use inappropriate language. If asked, I would tell you I was a good person. Why did I feel like I needed God?

My experience from hearing other people give their testimonies in church and on TV led me to believe you had be an alcoholic, drug addict, or a social outcast for Jesus to reach out and convict you to change your ways. I thought you had to be at the end of your rope with no place to turn before you asked for help from God. I was none of those things. I was a young teenage boy who was on a weeklong break from fall football practice having fun with his friends. Yet, sitting there on the slightly damp dew-laden ground, I felt the need for God in my life.

As I rationalized my feelings, I began to question my experience. Why did I feel such a strong need for God? I wasn't a bad person. I didn't feel the need to fall down on my knees and ask for the grace of God to help me overcome the sin in my life. I considered myself a good person. I had a good life. To be honest, I had no idea I would change my life that night, or that it even needed changing.

Since I didn't match any of the preconceived images I had stored in my mind of the people who desperately needed God, one question began to dominate my mind. Because I wasn't a "bad" person, would God even listen to my prayer? Would He be so busy helping other people my prayer would go unheard? Would I be placed on a waiting list for the next available representative? I was confident God was too busy helping people who needed Him much more than I did to be listening to me.

With uncertainty about what would happen next, I bowed my head and closed my eyes. With little fanfare nor voices booming from heaven in the background, I asked Jesus into my heart.

I wish I could adequately explain what happened next. I would like to tell you the sky opened up and angels of God descended from heaven to speak to me, but this didn't happen. I wish I could tell you a bright beam of light from heaven spotlighted me in the crowd to let others know about the decision I had just made to follow Jesus, but this didn't happen either. I wish I could tell you something fantastic happened when I prayed to God – Super Bowl halftime approved – but it didn't.

Instead, while sitting alone in a crowd of a hundred other teenagers, I felt a heavy weight being lifted from my shoulders, a weight I didn't even know I was carrying. The sense of aloneness I was feeling went away. A calm feeling overcame me as I felt the presence of God surround me. By the grace of God, sitting in the darkness of the night, I realized I needed a savior. And when I reached out to Him, He touched me.

We don't have to be bad people to need the grace of God. We don't need to have a made for TV movie experience to validate our relationship with Jesus. However we come to the realization we need God in our lives, He is always waiting for us – good people and bad – to call out His name and become children of God. Romans 3:23 says, *"For all have sinned and fall short of the glory of God."*

Sin is defined as anything which separates us from, or builds a barrier between us and the love of God. When we erect barriers, we detach ourselves from God and the relationship He wants to have with us. When we separate ourselves from God, we not only separate ourselves in the present, we isolate ourselves from Him for eternity.

We are only fooling ourselves if we think we are sinless and don't need the love of God in our lives. In 1 John 1:8 it says, *"If we claim to be without sin, we deceive ourselves and the truth is not in us."* We have all disappointed God no matter how good or bad we think we are. We all need God's grace and love. We all need the relationship He so freely gives.

When the campfire service ended, we quietly walked back to a small concession area for a snack and a little free time before returning to our cabins for the night. Adrenaline raced through my body like never before. I'm not sure I have ever been so excited about life. I wish I could have captured that feeling. I wish I could have put the hope and excitement I felt that night into a bottle and give away samples. I wish everyone could feel like I did the night I accepted Jesus Christ as my Lord and Savior.

I couldn't wait to tell my friends about the decision I made. I wanted to share the love God had shown to me sitting by the campfire. I wanted to tell them how I felt when He cleaned the slate of my sins. I wanted them to feel the same way I did. I was on fire for God and I wanted to share my experience with everyone at the camp and tell them Jesus was Lord of my life!

As I lay in my bunk bed, I had trouble going to sleep. My mind raced as I pondered the implication of my decision to follow Jesus Christ. How would my life change? What would my family back home think about what happened to me? How would my friends who weren't at the camp respond to me? As I prayed myself to sleep, I asked God to help me through the trials I would soon face.

The following night, I walked the aisle at the end of our nightly service during the invitation. Pastors from the various churches who brought teenagers to the camp stood at the front to receive anyone who had a decision to share. I couldn't wait to step into the aisle to share my decision with everyone.

But before I tell you what happened next, here is the rub of the story. I was Methodist. I attended the local Methodist church in my hometown. In fact, my parents were charter members of this church. I was at a Baptist church camp. My Methodist church was rather small by most standards and didn't provide many of the opportunities offered by the larger Baptist churches in town. Because my best friend and his family were members of one of the sponsoring churches for the camp, I went with him as a guest.

As I sat in my chair during the service – committed to sharing my decision – I struggled with which pastor I would tell my news. Although I was a guest of my friend's church, I didn't really know his pastor very well. He seemed to be a great guy. What little time I had spent with him, he had always been friendly to me. However, I wasn't even sure he knew my name. I thought a decision of this magnitude should be shared with someone you know really well, but my Methodist pastor was not at the camp. What was I going to do?

The moment the invitation started, I stepped into the aisle. Not knowing what was about to happen, I prayed to God as I walked forward to give me a sign and show me with whom I should share my decision. By the time I got to the front of the open air chapel (yes, Methodists sit on the back row too) every pastor was praying with someone except for one man. It wasn't my friend's pastor. It was someone I barely knew. He was the father of one of my school friends, Rev. Tom McDowell.

Accepting his availability as my sign from God, I took his outstretched hand, grasped it firmly, and told Rev. McDowell about my decision. Little did I know at the time, his availability for me was a much bigger sign from heaven than I expected. You see, the following year at the same church camp his daughter – my friend – and I made a connection. Although we had known each other since the fourth grade, we never had any real attraction toward each other. We were just good friends. But at camp the following year something changed. We started looking at each other differently. We began dating. I guess you could say it was a match made in heaven. Since then, Mary and I have always been together. We have been married for over 38 years and a couple for over 44 years. I can't imagine my life without her by my side.

Till this day, Rev. Tom McDowell is still one of the godliest men I know. He is a light of the world God continues to use even today at the age of 83. Little did I know when I first shook his hand and shared my decision, he would become my father-in-law some seven years later. When you pray to God and believe, anything and everything is possible. Jesus said in Matthew 21:22, *"If you believe, you will receive whatever you ask for in prayer."*

When we proclaim Jesus Christ as our Lord and Savior and become a child of God, all limits on our lives are removed. Anything is possible. You should prepare yourself to be amazed at the power of God and His love.

We also realize, maybe for the first time, our existence is not just a random occurrence of the universe, a freak accident of nature. We understand we are here for a reason, an overall purpose God has for all His people. More to the point, we realize God has a unique purpose for each of us to fulfill in His overall plan.

2

Why Am I Here?

Why am I here? Over the years I have asked myself this question thousands of times. In fact, this question has been pondered by some of the greatest minds in the world (mine not included) for centuries. Their answers are as varied as the colors of the rainbow. However, I believe there is only one right answer. We are here because of God's love. When God created the world He did it for only one reason: His desire to have a lasting relationship with us.

To make this possible, He first had to create a place for us to live. In just six days as described in the first chapter of Genesis God created the heavens

11

and the earth, gave the world light and darkness, and created the sky to separate the waters. He separated the land from the seas and covered the ground with seed bearing vegetation. He created the sun and the moon, the birds in the sky, and all types of creatures in the seas. Finally, He created livestock, creatures who move along the ground, and all the wild animals.

With everything in place and ready for us to inhabit the world, He created mankind in His own image, and blessed them. He encouraged them to be fruitful and increase in number, fill the earth, and subdue it. He created mankind to oversee and rule over all the creatures in the sea and in the sky, over the livestock and the wild animals, and the creatures that move along the ground. When God was finished, He saw what He created and it was good.

On the seventh day, God rested from all the work He had done. He blessed the seventh day and made it holy.

What a loving God! He loved us so much He created an entire universe where we could dwell; a beautiful place to live with others like us. A place with all the resources needed to sustain our lives.

Even today, because of our lack of complete knowledge, we still cannot fathom the complexity of detail which went into the creation of our universe so we might exist and have a relationship with Him. For example, our sun is just the right distance from Earth. A few miles closer to the sun and earth would be a fireball. A few miles farther away and earth would be a block of ice.

We need oxygen to exist. God created a system where trees take carbon dioxide – a substance which can kill us – and turns it into the life sustaining oxygen we need to live. Without trees, we would surely die.

The sun emits harmful radiation that will kill us. What did God do to protect us? He created a magnetic field generated from the core of the Earth which surrounds our planet and blocks the dangerous radiation from reaching Earth.

These are just three examples of how God demonstrated His love for us. However, there are thousands more examples we know about and many more we haven't yet discovered. It is mindboggling how God has shown His love for us through His design of the universe.

But back to the original question: Why are we here? Why did God go to so much trouble for us? As a loving parent, God loves us completely. God made a perfect place for mankind to live because of His love for us and His desire to be in a relationship with His children. He wants us to love Him so He can share His perfect love with us and – through us – show His unconditional love to the entire world. Despite what philosophers and scholars may have said in the past, this is the reason we are here: We are here because of God's love.

When my wife Mary and I decided to have children, it was because of this same kind of love. Although our love is not perfect like God's love for His children, it is a love only a parent can understand. It is a love which desires to create a home and environment where our children can feel safe and secure.

I can remember the birth of both my children vividly. For Jonathan – our first born – it was a whirlwind experience. It happened so fast, my wife and I almost missed it. Thinking we had all the time in the world to get to the hospital once my wife's contractions started, we didn't get excited. Our doctor assured us, since it was our first child, we had plenty of time.

Despite our doctor's reassurances, God had another plan for our son. God created Jonathan with little patience and he overruled the wisdom of our doctor and accelerated the pace of his delivery. My wife's contractions quickly went to five minutes apart – our signal to leave for the hospital – and one contraction later, jumped to two minutes. The next thing I remember is driving down the highway at over 100 mph with my four-way flashers blinking. Less than 20 minutes later, we screeched up in front of the emergency room entrance with my wife's feet propped up on the dashboard trying to resist the urge to push Jonathan out into the floorboard of our car.

Lucky for us there was a nurse getting off work and leaving the hospital as we arrived. She immediately stepped in to help and escorted my wife to the maternity ward while I went to park the car. Just like in the game of Monopoly® things happened so fast my wife didn't get to pass Go or collect $200, but bypassed the labor room and went directly to delivery. Within minutes, Jonathan was born.

Kristen – our second child – unlike Jonathan was in no hurry. Of course, because of our doctor's knowledge of Jonathan's birth, we were told to go straight to the hospital as soon as contractions began. Neither we nor our doctor wanted to take any chances this time around.

However, like before, God had another plan. Kristen was content. She was comfortable – despite my wife's discomfort – and was not ready to venture out into the new world. So, we sat and waited.

Worse yet, my wife's younger brother was to be married the following day. Between my wife crying over missing her brother's wedding and the hours of perfectly timed contractions, it was a very long day. In fact, to pass the time and help Mary get her mind off the wedding, I made a game out of her labor contractions. With the second hand on my wristwatch, I began to count down the next contraction like it was a NASA launch. 10...9...8...7...6...5... start all engines...4...3... commence breathing...2...1... contraction! With few exceptions, her labor monitor spiked showing a contraction in progress. In fact, if you closed your eyes and listened to the sound of my wife's controlled breathing – something she learned in Lamaze class – it sounded like you were really at an official NASA launch. Many, many launch simulations and hours later we finally met Kristen.

I cannot describe how I felt the exact moment each child was born. Until then, I didn't believe in love at first sight. How could anyone love someone the first time they see them? The birth of my two children changed my thinking.

The moment I saw Jonathan and Kristen my heart melted. Let me put it this way. I have known my wife since the fourth grade. We became good friends and started dating in the 11th grade. We dated for six years before we got married. We didn't have Jonathan until four years after we were married. By this time I had known my wife for over 18 years and had grown to love her completely. But the instant each child was born, I had the same love for them as I had for Mary. It didn't take years to develop this love. It was immediate. I loved both of my children completely!

So is God's love for us. He loves us immediately. He loves us completely! Even if you are perceived in the world as the result of an unloving marriage, a violent crime, or a mistake, nothing could be further from the truth. God doesn't make mistakes. God doesn't have accidents. You were no accident. God loves you like He loves all his children. The Bible says in Ephesians 1:4 (MSG), *"Long before he laid down earth's foundations, he had us in mind, had settled on us as the focus of his love, to be made whole and holy by his love."* God made you so He can share His love with you. He made your life so you could fulfill a purpose in His grand plan for the universe.

As much as we may think our lives and jobs are insignificant to God's plans, they're not. We all have jobs which contribute to a greater purpose. And although we may feel our contribution is inconsequential, we each play a vital role in making God's greater plan possible. No matter how underappreciated we may feel in the role we play, the purpose we fulfill is vital to its success.

For a few minutes consider the lowest paid entry level position in the company where you work. What would happen if this person didn't take their job seriously and didn't perform their duties as required by the position? I suspect over time, if they were not being performed properly, the tasks they are responsible for would begin to clog the bigger wheel of the organization. For example, the garbage wouldn't be collected and trash would begin to pile up in the office. The mail wouldn't get delivered and important letters and customer requests wouldn't be properly attended to. The switchboard wouldn't be answered and important calls would be missed. Whether you are the CEO of your company or hold an entry level position, every position plays an important role in the overall success of your organization and contributes to a greater purpose.

Being a child of God under the leadership of the greatest CEO in the universe is no different. God created you with a unique role in mind, with a greater purpose to accomplish. Although you may think your role or purpose in God's overall plan is insignificant, it's not. Just like an organization depends on every employee to meet the overall goals of the company, God depends on each of his children to contribute to the overall purpose of mankind using the unique gifts, passions, and tools each of us has been given. The Bible says in 2 Timothy 2:20-21, *"In a large house there are articles not only of gold and silver, but also of wood and clay; some are for special purposes and some for common use. Those who cleanse themselves from the latter will be instruments for special purposes, made holy, useful to the Master and prepared to do any good work."*

It is only human nature that we want to have an important job. We want a job people respect. We want a position where people admire our abilities and generously reward us for our hard work. Who doesn't want to be the CEO of a company, the chief engineer of a research department, or the coach of the most successful sports program in the country? Isn't this what we all strive to be in our chosen fields? Don't we all want to be superstars?

Unfortunately, we all can't be superstars. Although some of us rise to the top of our fields, most of us don't. In my case, I would love to have the speaking skills of a Billy Graham or an Andy Stanley, but I don't. I would do almost anything to have the writing skills of a Rick Warren, but by now you know I don't. (smile) I deeply desire to have the faith of Paul, but more often than not I'm more like Thomas. As such, many of us are in jobs where we feel underappreciated, underpaid, and unfulfilled.

However, just because we are not getting the respect or appreciation we think we should be receiving, we should never be discouraged. The reason for the discontentment we feel is not based on our job or the responsibilities assigned to us, but is incorrectly centered on how the world values the work we do.

Because of the devil's influence in the world, he has distorted our value system and turned it upside down. He makes us believe someone with a .257 batting average is worth more than a policeman or fireman. He makes us believe a person with a tech idea who has never made a profit is somehow more valuable than a teacher or a doctor. He makes us falsely believe how many likes we get on something we post to social media determines how much we are loved and respected. Nothing could be further from the truth! The reason for our discontentment is not based on the job we perform. It is based on the value the world has wrongly placed on positions within our society which we have bought into and believe.

To value our work as God designed it, we must turn away from the world's value system and look to God for our worth, our respect, and appreciation. All God's children are loved and important. From the unemployed, disabled, and entry level positions to the president of the United States, God has given each of us unique gifts and talents to be used to complete His will – our reason for living – in the world. Only when we focus on God's value system do we see the significance we bring to every job we perform.

How do you stay focused on the purpose God has given you in His overall plan? Follow these three truths. First, whatever you do, dedicate your work to the Lord. God has designed you for a unique purpose which contributes to His overall plans. When you dedicate your work to God, He helps you find your purpose and allows you to use your gifts as they were designed to be used. In Proverbs 16:3 it says, *"Commit to the Lord whatever you do and he will establish your plans."* Whatever you do, trust God and He will make your work rewarding.

Second, when you commit your work to the Lord, He will help you determine your path. The Bible says in Proverbs 16:9, *"In their hearts humans plan their course, but the Lord establishes their steps."* When you leave God out of the planning, your reason for living gets lost in the noise of life and you miss opportunities God has planned for you to experience. Stay focused on God. Trust Him to determine your next steps so you will always stay on task, completing the purpose the Lord has given you to complete.

Finally, when you include God in your planning, you will succeed. Proverbs 16:20 says, *"Whoever gives heed to instruction prospers, and blessed is the one who trusts in the Lord."* Trusting God with your work and letting Him plan your steps ensures success. As Isaiah tells us in Chapter 14, verse 24, *"The Lord Almighty has sworn, Surely, as I have planned, so it will be, and as I have purposed, so it will happen."*

What happens when we don't include the Lord in our plans? The Bible warns us in Isaiah 29:15, *"Woe to those who go to the great depths to hide their plans from the Lord, who do their work in darkness and think, who sees us? Who will know?"* When we do this, we lose. We miss out on all the blessings God had prepared for us. God doesn't need us to accomplish His goals in the universe. He can do anything and His purpose will always prevail over what we plan in our own hearts. The Bible says in Proverbs 19:21, *"Many are the plans in a person's heart, but it is the Lord's purpose that prevails."* Staying focused on God assures our plans are God's plans and we reap all the blessings the Lord has in store for us.

Declaring Jesus Christ as your Lord and Savior and becoming aware of a greater purpose is a call to action that shouldn't be taken lightly. God – our father – wants to be in a loving relationship with us – His children. He dreamed of our birth before we were even conceived. He created our universe so we would have a place to live. He formed and designed each of us in our mother's womb for a purpose to complete.

God has a plan for your life. His plan for the world includes you. Keep your eyes focused on God and do what you were created to do and His plan for you – your reason for living – will be accomplished.

God's love is good! God's love is perfect! We are here because of God's Love and His desire to be in a relationship with us.

3

How Do I Build A Relationship With God?

To build a relationship with God, we must make time to talk to Him. It is impossible to have a strong or lasting relationship with anyone, especially God, if we don't make time to talk to and be with Him.

I love my children. I love being around them and talking with them about their worries, dreams, and hopes for the future. As a parent, who doesn't? We want our children to come to us and seek our counsel.

My son's dreams haven't changed much over the years. Jonathan has been obsessed with how things work from an early age. He filled his craving for knowledge by asking questions at every opportunity and tearing things apart.

Because of Jonathan's fascination with how things work, he had very few nice toys. His need to understand the interworking's of each one led him to tearing his toys apart soon after he got them. As a result, instead of beautiful, functioning toys which would perhaps become valuable one day, he had boxes and boxes of parts from the toys he destroyed learning every detail about how they worked.

My daughter Kristen was totally different. She had little interest in how things worked. She was more interested in building relationships. From the moment she was born she began making friends with everyone. In fact, my wife and I were so concerned Kristen would go home with a complete stranger, we kept a close eye on her when we were in public. Despite repeatedly telling Kristen not to talk to people she didn't know, she knew no strangers. In her mind, everyone was her friend.

In spite of our children's differences in how they approached life, Mary and my relationship with our children grew and developed similarly over the years. As babies, both children depended on us for everything. They trusted us completely and nothing was done without our involvement.

As young children Jonathan and Kristen slowly began to push us away wanting to do everything for themselves. For example, they wanted to pick the clothes they wore, how they combed their hair, and the time they went to bed at night. They not only asked for more involvement in the decision making process, they demanded it.

As teenagers, they went from tolerating our existence to not wanting to be seen with us. In their minds, they didn't need our help anymore. They knew everything and pushed us away when we offered our help.

As time went on – I don't really know the exact moment when it happened – Jonathan and Kristen slowly started coming back to us for assistance. They began to need us again. They wanted our opinion. We were no longer shunned by them, but were included in their lives and were consulted on important decisions.

As adults, we are friends. Although Mary and I will always be their parents, today we are much more than just their mother and father. We're friends too. Our relationship with Jonathan and

Kristen continues to grow, deeper than ever before. To be honest, I like this phase of our relationship better than all the others combined!

When we become children of God, our relationship with God also changes over time. In the beginning when we first accept Him as our Lord and Savior and become a baby Christian, we trust God with all our heart. We feel the love of God and we love Him as completely as we know how.

Over time, with false encouragement from the world, we allow our focus to turn away from God and we begin to neglect Him by thinking we can handle everything ourselves. Maybe a prayer went unanswered or something wasn't resolved like we thought it should, and we start to drift away. Some of us even go as far as completely turning our backs on God.

Then, something happens. It could be a tragedy, an illness, a death in the family, or anything else which causes us to realize we are not in control of the universe. I call it the "hit between the eyes with a two-by-four" moment. Something happens and we know we need God's help to take back control of our lives. It wakes us from our indifference to God and rekindles our relationship with Him.

No one wants to go through these types of experiences. No one wants to be reminded of our need for God with a tragedy or an illness. How do we avoid the "two-by-four" moments and build and maintain a lasting relationship with God? We do it the same way we build a lifelong relationship with our best friend.

Think about one of your best friends. How did your relationship with them grow into something special? I'll tell you how. You were so close to them some people would say you were attached at the hip to each other. You stayed in constant contact with them and never let them out of your sight for long. You shared your deepest secrets, fears, and dreams with each other. You went to your friend for advice when you didn't know what to do. That's how two people become best friends.

Building a strong relationship with God is no different. Just like a child and a parent build a relationship with each other or a friend becomes a best friend over time, we must have the same kind of relationship with God. We must become attached to Him and never let Him out of our sight. We must share our deepest secrets, fears, and dreams with Him. We must continually seek His guidance in all things. To have the lasting relationship we all seek with God, He must not only be our father, He must also become our best friend!

How do you become best friends with God? Just like you do with your best earthly friend, you talk to Him. You pray to Him. But more than just talk and pray, you listen. You allow God to speak to you. Like a best friend, you develop a two-way relationship with God which allows Him to give you the guidance and support you need in your life.

Jesus teaches us how to pray to God in Matthew 6:6-13. Jesus tells us we should start by praying to God in private. We can't build a lasting relationship with our best friend by baring our soul in public, nor can we with God. To build a strong relationship with God we have to talk to Him, one-on-one in private. We have to go to Him in secret and show Him our heart.

Second, Jesus tells us to keep our prayer short and to the point. Using superfluous language or repeating ourselves doesn't impress our best friend or God. He knows what we are going to pray even before we begin. There's no reason to puff up our requests to impress Him. Like any best friend, He knows our heart and loves us no matter what we tell Him.

Third, we are told to pray directly to God praising His holy name. Jesus assures us God is always waiting and will be there for us when we call upon His name. Like a best friend who will drop whatever they are doing to answer our call, God is no different.

However, God is much more than just a best friend. He is the creator of the universe and He has promised us eternal life with Him. With gratitude, we should often tell Him we believe His promise and look forward to our time with Him throughout eternity.

Just as God promised us eternal life, He also promised to meet our every need. Jesus taught us we shouldn't be afraid to ask God for anything. Although we should never disrespect God by asking Him to supply unnecessary wants, we should openly talk to Him about giving us everything we need to accomplish our reason for living. God's promise assures our needs will be supplied as they are required. All we have to do is ask and trust He will provide.

Still, I need to make one thing unmistakably clear. Although possible, I'm not saying your prayers will be answered the moment you ask, or your prayers will be answered in the way you want them to be answered. However, I will tell you God is a loving God who has perfect knowledge of the future and how His plan – your life's purpose – is to be completed in the world. If you take your concerns to God and trust Him, He will answer your prayers and meet your needs in a way which will allow you to fulfill the life purpose He has created for you to complete. All you have to do is talk to God and listen.

Fourth, Jesus teaches us we are to pray that God's plan – God's purpose for our lives – will be completed on earth and in heaven. In our conversations with God, we should praise Him for giving each of us a reason for living and allowing us to be a part of His plan.

Fifth, Because of our sinful nature, Jesus reminds us we are to ask God to forgive us of our sins and forgive those who sin against us. God loves us so much He was willing to let His only Son die on a cross to erase our sins forever. Likewise, in the spirit of God's love, we must also forgive those who sin against us.

Finally, we are taught by Jesus it's OK to ask God not to give us trials so harsh it causes us to lose faith in Him. 1 Corinthians 10:13 teaches, *"God is faithful; he will not let you be tempted beyond what you can bear. But when you are tempted, he will also provide a way out so that you can endure it."* Paul tells us we should pray that God will show grace toward us and never give us more than we can bear.

In addition, throughout the Bible great men of God have given us further insight on how we should talk to God. In 1 Timothy 2:1 we are told to pray for all people, not just ourselves. Just as we pray to God about our needs, we must also lift up the needs of others. Interceding for others shows our love for our neighbor, God's second most important commandment.

In 1 Thessalonians 5:17, we are told to pray continually giving thanks in all things. Instead of praying at defined times, we are to be in con- tinuous conversation with God. Just like with any best friend, if you only talk to them occasionally, they won't be your best friend very long. We have to keep in constant contact with them to build a strong relationship. God wants to have the same kind of relationship with us as we have with our best friend.

In Ephesians 5:20, we are taught to give thanks to God in all things. Most of us have lived long enough to know everything is not always going to go our way. There are going to be times in all our lives when the world seems like it is piling on top of us. When life happens, we are to praise God and thank Him at every opportunity for giving us trials which will prepare us to accomplish our reason for living. Romans 8:28 says, *"And we know that in all things God works for the good of those who love him, who have been called according to his purpose."*

How is your relationship with God? Are you building a relationship with Him that will stand the test of time? Can you say God and you are best friends? Do something right now. Pray to God, using the example Jesus gave us, and bare your soul. He wants to be your best friend. He wants you to be successful fulfilling the life purpose He has designed just for you. God is waiting to talk to you.

4

How Did God Prepare Me For What He Created Me to Do?

When the Bible describes God creating the world in seven days, a lot of details were obviously left out. Creating a world with the complexities necessary for everything to work as it should in just seven days is perhaps the most understated event in the history of mankind.

The human body is a good example of this complexity. It has been studied for thousands of years and we don't know, nor will we possibly ever know, everything about God's design. Ecclesiastes 11:5 says, *"As you do not know the path of the wind, or how the body is formed in a mother's womb, so you cannot understand the work of God, the Maker of all things."*

Although we do not have complete knowledge of our bodies, everything we understand at this time seems to point back to our deoxyribonucleic acid (DNA) as the basic building block of our design. According to scientists, DNA is a molecule which holds the genetic instructions of all living organisms known to man. Some have called it the God code.

God's code is at work and in control of every child from the moment of conception. And, within nanoseconds of its birth, this little person's DNA begins to communicate to us – as crudely as it may be – what he or she is thinking by the way it cries, the expressions on its face, and through its body language. Without being able to talk, the child begins to tell to us what has been programmed into its DNA.

Both my children had strong genetics. Although my children's DNA came from the same parents, they were two completely different people with different likes and dislikes. For example, Jonathan never wanted to sleep. He was afraid he would miss something if he closed his eyes. As a result, Jonathan fought with all his strength to stay awake. Kristen, on the other hand, loved to sleep. You could lay her down in her bed and she would be asleep within minutes. She never moved until she woke up the next morning.

Like their sleep patterns, their food preferences were just as strongly programmed into their DNA. When they started eating baby food, they immediately knew what they liked and didn't like. Some foods were liked so much they held their mouths wide-open like a baby bird waiting for its mother to feed them a big juicy worm. They grunted and kicked their little feet in anticipation of every spoonful.

Other foods had a completely opposite reaction. For Jonathan it was creamed carrots. He hated them. From the very first spoonful he tasted, he spit them out as soon as they went into his mouth. For Kristen it was spinach. She would literally turn around in her highchair to avoid the spoon being shoved into her mouth. It was obvious from the moment Jonathan and Kristen were introduced to these foods they didn't like them. They got angry when we tried to feed them these foods.

How could two children's distinctive likes and dislikes be so developed at birth? How could two children sharing the genes of the same parents be so different? I think we have to look at our DNA more closely to understand.

Our bodies contain around 50 trillion cells.[1] Each cell has a complete set of instructions programmed into it through our DNA that determine who we are, what we look like, and the traits we have. DNA is essential to our existence.

Our DNA is organized into chromosomes, genes, and genetic switches. All humans have 23 pairs of chromosomes. Half come from the mother and half from the father. These 23 pairs of chromosomes have been handed down to us from generation to generation since the beginning of time. In fact, all living things have chromosomes organizing their DNA. For example, a dog has 39 pairs of chromosomes, a horse has 32, a cow has 30, a mango has 20, and a radish has nine.

Chromosomes are further organized into genes. Each cell in our body contains around 20,000 to 25,000 genes.[2] Think of our DNA as the cookbook. Our genes are the recipes which determine how each cell works together to give us our traits.[3] Although all of us have the same set of genes, variations in how our genes are organized explain the differences we have from one another. For example, if someone has red hair, a bubbling personality, and a love of homemade apple pie, it is because of the genes they inherited from their parents and how those genes are organized within their cells.

Our cells use the recipes written in our genes to make proteins. These proteins do much of the work of the cells. They give each cell their shape and structure, determine their function within our bodies, and give our cells direction on how to behave. For example, a cell could be programmed to be a brain cell, an ear, liver, or something totally different. Whatever the cell's recipe tells it to make or do is what the cell becomes.

As you might imagine, there are many different types of cells – about 200 – which make up our bodies.[4] There are bone cells, blood cells, skin cells, kidney cells, and many others. Controlling these cells is a complex system of master genetic switches turning genes on and off, making sure the right proteins are made at the right time in each cell.[5]

Working together the chromosomes, genes, and genetic switches control our DNA and determine who we are, the traits we have, the passions that drive us, and the purpose our God-given gifts and tools were intended to fulfill. This is why understanding our DNA – the DNA code God has given each of us – is vital to determining the direction our lives were intended to travel, realizing the successes we were meant to have, and living the lives God intended for us to live.

What has God coded you to do? How do you think the programming God has given you through your DNA has affected your choices, your path in life? Not until we spend time with God and understand the programming He has given each of us through our DNA – God's code – can we fully realize the unique life purpose God has given each of us, and do what God has created us to do. The Bible teaches us in Proverbs 3:5-6, *"Trust in the* LORD *with all your heart and lean not on your own understanding; in all your ways submit to him, and he will make your paths straight."*

Now that we understand a little more about how God programs our DNA to create the person we've become, it's time to look at how God's code sets the direction of our lives. Before we are even conceived, God is planning the direction He wants our lives to take. Once determined, God uses two people – a man and woman – who best match his requirements to form the exact genetic code He needs us to have to fulfill our life's purpose. At conception, God forms our little bodies through our DNA code to give us the traits, gifts, and passions needed to accomplish the responsibilities and tasks He has designed for us to complete. Even before we are conceived, God has already set the direction of our lives, according to His plan. Understanding our unique God-given purpose and walking the path He has determined for us to follow is essential to the relationship He wants to have with us and to reap the true sustaining happiness – the joy – God intended for our lives. The Bible says in 2 Corinthians 5:5, *"Now the one who has fashioned us for this very purpose is God, who has given us the Spirit as a deposit, guaranteeing what is to come."*

My son Jonathan's direction in life was set at conception. Really, it was. He has always had an aptitude for math. In fact, he was doing simple math problems even as a toddler. However, not until he took his first advanced math course in middle school, did my wife and I really understand how Jonathan's DNA was working to determine his future.

Early in the year, my wife and I were asked by Jonathan's math teacher to come to a conference to discuss his work. Unexpectedly in the meeting, Jonathan's teacher accused him of cheating. According to Mr. Smith, although Jonathan had never been caught cheating, there could be no other explanation for his perfect scores.

Spreading Jonathan's tests on the table in front of us, he presented his evidence. Like a New York lawyer, one by one he revealed his case showing us the reasons for his conclusion. Each test displayed two numerical columns. In the left column, the answers were numbered one through whatever. The right column contained what looked like random numbers. As Mr. Smith explained, the column of random numbers had the correct answers to the problems on the test. Because Jonathan didn't show the steps necessary to get to the correct answers, he surmised Jonathan must be cheating.

Mary and I sat in silence not knowing how to respond. Jonathan knew our stance on cheating and the dire consequences he would face if he did. We made it very clear to both our children cheating was not acceptable. We left the conference promising to talk with Jonathan to find out what was going on.

Sitting at our kitchen table after supper, my wife and I replayed our conversation with Mr. Smith and prepared to confront Jonathan with the evidence we were given during the parent-teacher conference. Mr. Smith, although convinced Jonathan was cheating, made a statement during our discussions which stuck in our minds. He said, "not only did Jonathan write down the correct answers to all the test problems without showing his work, he also wrote down the correct answers to bonus questions on problems not yet covered in class." We thought: how could Jonathan be cheating on math problems not covered in class he shouldn't know how to do?

Looking Jonathan in the eye, we spread his test papers in front of him on the table and confronted him with Mr. Smith's concerns. Jonathan never blinked an eye and proceeded to explain to us it was a waste of time to show his work when he could just look at the problem and know the answer. He thought Mr. Smith was being unreasonable to ask him to show his work.

Relieved Jonathan wasn't cheating we verified his explanation by presenting him with multiple math problems we made up. Writing down an algebraic problem on a piece of paper, we asked Jonathan to give us the answer while Mary and I solved the problem through the traditional method.

To our amazement, Jonathan quickly blurted out the answer before we could decipher the problem on paper or in a calculator. As you might imagine, we sat speechless with our mouths open wide.

As promised, we followed up with Mr. Smith the following morning and shared our findings and asked him to confirm our conclusion. Later that afternoon, Mr. Smith called us with childlike excitement to confirm our findings. For the next several weeks, Mr. Smith, Mary, and I worked hard to convince Jonathan that showing his work was important to the process of checking his answers as he encountered even more advanced math problems. This was not an easy sell.

To say Jonathan has a thing for math is an understatement. He has a gift, a God-given gift. His chromosomes, genes, and genetic switches have programed his DNA in such a way math comes easily to him.

But not only is Jonathan good at math, he has a passion for math. When his class went to the library, He checked out math books to read in his spare time. When our family went on vacation, instead of taking comic books or something more age appropriate to read, Jonathan took books on advanced math subjects he had never seen. His gift, his passion for math drove him, and with time, became his life's purpose.

Although Jonathan's specific gift may be math, we all have gifts and passions programmed into our DNA by God that are the basis for fulfilling our life's purpose, His intended plan for our lives. It is up to us to embrace who we are, and with God's help, find the reason He created us. Ephesians 1:11 says, *"In him we were also chosen, having been predestined according to the plan of him who works out everything in conformity with the purpose of his will."* When we understand how our DNA is programmed by God, we find our reason for living, God's plan for our lives.

However, knowing our reason for living is not always obvious. Most of us don't realize or find what God created us to do as easily as my son Jonathan. For him it was evident he had a gift for math at a very early age. In fact, even before his mom and I fully realized his gift, Jonathan had already embraced his direction in life and started pursuing his passion for numbers.

Jonathan seemed to know what he wanted to do with his life even before he started school. When he was 3 years old, he began to verbalize his desire to become an astronaut or a pilot. As he got older, his continued fascination with flight and his aptitude for math drove his every thought. He was passionate about these subjects and he wanted to know everything about them. Eventually, his passion led him to his career as an aerospace engineer and his reason for living became clear to everyone.

Mary's love of music is very similar to Jonathan's love of math. Like Jonathan, Mary's passion for music started at an early age and it grew over time and eventually led to her career. In fact, because of her love of music, I tell our friends she thinks in whole notes and quarter notes. Even today, as a retired public school music teacher, her entire life revolves around her love of music.

Regrettably for most of us, our reason for living is not as apparent as it is for my son or wife. Most of us spend our entire lives going from one thing to another searching for the happiness that seems to elude us. My daughter Kristen and I fall into this description. Both of us have spent most of our lives looking for the passion we see in others. We've both changed jobs multiple times over the years looking for our reason for living.

Why do so many of us have so much trouble finding our path in life? Is it because God didn't give us any gifts or passions? Did God only give a life's purpose to some of us? Absolutely not; each of us has gifts and passions programmed into our DNA by God to be used to carry out His grand plan for our lives. The Bible says in 1 Corinthians 12:4-6, *"There are different kinds of gifts, but the same Spirit distributes them. There are different kinds of service, but the same Lord. There are different kinds of working, but in all of them and in everyone it is the same God at work."*

So why is it so difficult for some of us to find our reason for living? I think there are two main reasons. First, just as God gave us our traits, gifts, and passions through our DNA, He also gave us free will to choose the direction our lives eventually take. Although God gave us all the tools we need to be successful in life and find the joy He intended for us to experience, He also gave us the right to reject His plan for our lives and allows us to choose the path our lives ultimately take. *This is what the Lord says: "Stand at the crossroads and look; ask for the ancient paths, ask where the good way is, and walk in it, and you will find rest for your souls."* (Jeremiah 6:16)

When we ignore God's plan for our lives, we miss out on all the joy, success, and happiness He wants us to have.

Did Kristen and I purposefully dismiss God's plan for our lives? Not at all! I can't speak for Kristen or the "two-by-four" moment which helped her realize her reason for living, but in my case I didn't turn my back on God. Instead, I didn't actively seek His leadership. I was afraid of what God might ask me to do. As a result, I didn't realize what God created me to do until I was in my 50s.

When we don't seek God's leadership in our lives, sometimes the joy, success, and happiness meant for us by God is replaced with disappointment, failure, and misery. John 3:36 says, "*Whoever believes in the Son has eternal life, but whoever rejects the Son will not see life, for God's wrath remains on them.*" When we reject God, our real reason for living and joy are lost for eternity. We never see or experience the lives God intended for us to live.

Good news! It is never too late to return to God and seek His leadership. Like every parent who gets rejected by one of their children but still loves them, God loves us unconditionally. He wants to have a relationship with us and waits patiently for us to come back to Him. To realize what God created us to do and reap the rewards of following the path God intended for us to follow, we must actively seek Him and submit to His leadership.

The second reason we have trouble finding our purpose for living is we don't take the time necessary to discover and embrace the gifts, passions, and tools God has given us. We live in a busy world that thrives on chaos. When the gifts, passions, and tools given to us by God are not immediately clear, we must take the time to stop, remove ourselves from the chaos, and listen to God. We must eliminate our distractions as much as we can and examine the programming God has given us to fulfill our reason for living. The Bible teaches us in Proverbs 8:32-36, *"Now then, my children, listen to me; blessed are those who keep my ways. Listen to my instruction and be wise; do not disregard it. Blessed are those who listen to me, watching daily at my doors, waiting at my doorway. For those who find me find life and receive favor from the* LORD. *But those who fail to find me harm themselves; all who hate me love death."* When we listen to God, He blesses us by revealing our reason for living.

When we stay focused on God and actively seek the purpose He designed for us to fulfill, it allows us to concentrate on our real priorities and the things which will ultimately bring us the joy God intended for all of us to have in this life and for eternity. Choose God as He has chosen you and reap the rewards of what He has created you to do!

Endnotes

[1] 23andMe, "What Are Genes?," 23andMe, https://www.23andme.com/gen101/genes/

[2] U.S Department of Health & Human Services, "What is a gene?," Genetics Home Reference, USA.gov, http://ghr.nlm.nih.gov/handbook/basics/gene

[3] 23andMe, "What Are Genes?," 23andMe, https://www.23andme.com/gen101/genes/

[4] Advancing Science Serving Society (AAAS), "The Cells In Your Body," ScienceNetLinks.com, American Association for the Advancement of Science, http://sciencenetlinks.com/student-teacher-sheets/cells-your-body/

[5] 23andMe, "What Are Genes?," 23andMe, https://www.23andme.com/gen101/genes/

5

How Do I Determine God's Plan For My Life?

I wish we could look in the mirror and know exactly what God wants us to do with our lives. I wish there was a test we could take to tell us what God has in store for us. Unfortunately, it's not that simple. To truly understand what God created us to do we have to prayerfully focus on God and carefully examine our lives as He made us. When we embrace the unique tools God has given us through our DNA to be successful in our world and follow His leadership, we find our life's purpose and are able to focus on our priorities, simplify our lives, and live the lives God intended for us live.

As we look to God for direction, I think there are six ways to help us determine what God created us to do. As you go through this list, prayerfully consider each one and listen to God as He gives you direction about your life's purpose.

Through My Passions

We all have God-given passions programmed into our DNA to help us fulfill our reason for living. This programming is essential to God's plan for our lives and provides the drive needed to complete the tasks assigned to us by God.

According to Encarta Dictionary, a passion is an intense or overpowering emotion such as love, joy, hate, or anger. It can also be described as a strong liking or enthusiasm for a subject or activity. Being passionate can also mean having a keen interest or intense desire for something.

We all have passions. We all have strong emotional connections to something. When we explore the passions God gave us, it helps us better understand our life's purpose and God's plan for our lives.

Take me for example. I'm passionate about many things. I'm passionate about Disney and everything associated with the brand. The movies, the characters, the theme parks, and Disney's attention to detail put a smile on my face and excitement in my voice when I talk about them. Just typing the last sentence I felt a grin appear on my face. As crazy as this may sound, I consider Walt Disney World in Florida my heaven on Earth. Being there makes me happy, and although it brings pain to my wallet, it brings joy to my soul.

I'm also passionate about sports, especially football. When I say football, I really mean Alabama Crimson Tide football. In fact, I'm so crazy about the Tide I ran a website called Tide Tradition for several years so I could share my passion with others.

Why am I so passionate about Alabama football? I grew up in Alabama, and when you grow up in Alabama, you have to choose your allegiance as soon as you are able talk. As soon as you can verbalize Alabama or Auburn, you must choose "Roll Tide" or "War Eagle." The loyalty to the university you select runs deep and cuts across family ties. If someone from Alabama tells you they pull for both schools, they are lying to you. Rooting for both teams is neither possible nor allowed by state law.

I'm also passionate about writing and the creative process. The challenge of taking an idea and developing it into something others want to read is very rewarding to me. Although it is a skill I will never fully conquer, because of my passion for this art and my desire to do what God wants me to do, I work hard to improve the skills God has given me. It is something I struggle with daily.

But even more than Disney, Alabama football, or the creative process, I'm passionate about helping people find their God-given purpose, helping them simplify their lives, and helping them claim the life God intended for each of His children to live. As I get older and better understand the effects of aging on our bodies, I realize our window to do what God created us to do is very small and we have no time to waste. Life is too short not to be living our lives as it was intended to be lived. However, like I said before there is good news: it is never too late to start. So as you might imagine, I am passionate as well as motivated to help people live their lives as it was envisioned by God.

What are you passionate about? What gives you great personal satisfaction? If you had a message to share, who would you share it with and what would be the message? If asked to teach, what would you teach? If you were guaranteed to be successful, what would you pursue? If you could star in your own TV series or movie, what would it be about? When with others, what do you mostly want to talk about? If you had all the money in the world, how would you spend your time? If you could do anything, what would be your dream job? Pursuing the answers to these questions and others like them as you explore how God programmed your passions could change your life forever.

Paul was passionate. From the moment he met Jesus on the road to Damascus, he was on fire for Jesus. He traveled from town to town teaching about Jesus and Christianity to the Roman people and wrote 13 books of the New Testament. No one in history has contributed more to the Christian faith than Paul through his writings.

Joshua and Caleb were passionate. Following Moses from Egypt across the Red Sea into the wilderness they were selected with 10 other men to go and explore the Promised Land. After 40 days, they came back to Moses and reported the land was everything promised, flowing with milk and honey. But, because of the powerful people who controlled it, the Israelites were frightened and were not in favor of going to this new land. Because of the Israelite's unfaithfulness, God punished the Israelites in the wilderness for the next 40 years and everyone age 20 years or older, except for Joshua and Caleb, died. Their faithfulness and passion saved them and they both entered the Promised Land.

The prophet Jeremiah was passionate, despite the unpopular position in which God placed him. God sent Jeremiah to give the people of Judah their last warning to repent before He cast them out of Israel and placed them in captivity under the Babylonians. Jeremiah's passion for the Hebrew people, and his dedication to the mission God assigned him, led him to preach to the unyielding people of Israel for 40 years. No matter how hard Jeremiah tried to convince the people of Judah to turn away from their false gods, he could not change their hearts. Jeremiah became known as the "Weeping Prophet" for the tears he shed as he passionately preached God's word and visualized the impending destruction coming to the people of Judah.

Paul, Joshua, Caleb, and Jeremiah were all blessed with passions from God which helped define their purpose. You are no different. Just like these great leaders of the Bible, God has given you a passion to help you fulfill your reason for living. It could be passion for a forgotten cause needing support from your community. It could be a passion for a group of people who can't speak for themselves. It could be a passion for research to eliminate a particular disease. It could be a passion for feeding the homeless at your local shelter or providing meals to the elderly. It could be a passion for a public office or a small leadership role in your homeowners association. It could be a passion to be the best plumber or electrician in your city. Or, it could be like my passion to help people do what God created them to do. Whatever it may be, God has given you a passion to help you fulfill your life's purpose.

Take time to explore and understand your passions. My hope is you will learn something new about yourself, rediscover something you had forgotten, and refocus your life on the passion or passions which matter to you greatly. You were given these passions by God for a reason. Psalm

37:4 says, *"Take delight in the Lord, and he will give you the desires of your heart."* I pray you will allow God to make your passions come alive in your life and direct you to what He has designed you to do.

Through My Likes & Dislikes

My wife and I did something special three years ago for our 35th wedding anniversary. Normally, we go to dinner at a nice restaurant to celebrate another year of marriage. As mundane as this may seem, we've never been very big on giving gifts to each other. To be honest, we never thought it necessary. Being together and enjoying each other's company has always been enough. However, this year was different. Because of all the family turmoil surrounding my mother's serious illness, we waited.

Dealing with a family illness puts a tremendous strain on everyone involved. Traveling back and forth to Alabama from Kentucky to help my mom, dad, and other family members when they were at the end of their rope was stressful. Living seven hours away makes it almost impossible to make a significant contribution and deal with issues as they arise. In one short three day visit, I drove over 1,700 miles helping my mom and dad get to doctor appointments and run errands. Although I never carried the bulk of the load because of being so far away, it still took a tremendous toll on Mary and me.

A few weeks after my mother's passing, through the grace of God, things were more relaxed than they had been in months and Mary and I felt comfortable enough to go ahead and celebrate our anniversary. Mary suggested we go to a local dinner playhouse to see the musical *Mary Poppins*.

Going to the play was a perfect idea. It was a great evening. We shared our table with a cute couple about our age who kept us in stiches. They made us laugh like we hadn't laughed in months. Sharing the moment with our new friends, my beautiful wife sitting at my side, and enjoying the musical was just what the doctor ordered.

During the play I think Bert said it best. Do you remember Bert? He was played by Dick Van Dyke in the original 1964 *Mary Poppins* movie.[1] During the song Chim Chim Cher-Ee Bert told us, "I does what I likes and I likes what I do!"[2] He's right you know. We all have things we like to do, and if we pay attention to these things, they can give us clues about our reason for living.

I believe God programs our DNA with our likes and dislikes for a reason, to give us direction. Think about it. Why would one person like a tomato and another person not? Why do some of us like sports while others like basket weaving? Why do some of us like to travel while others of us would rather stay at home? Just as my wife likes music, my daughter likes animals of all kinds, and my son likes math, we all have things we like which drive us toward our passions and lead us to our reason for living.

What do you like? What puts a smile on your face or extra spring in your step? What gives you joy when nothing else will? What are you doing when you are the happiest? When you have time to do anything you want, what do you do? What activities make you lose track of time? Despite everything else going on in your life, when are you at peace? Answers to these questions and others like them may give you tangible paths to explore as you find the life God intended for you to live.

Simon Peter, Andrew, James, and John liked to fish. They loved going out in their boats and throwing their nets over the side. I'm sure, like all fishermen they had their favorite fishing holes and techniques they preferred over others based on years of trial and error. But everything changed when they met Jesus at the Sea of Galilee. *"Come follow me"* Jesus said, and they immediately left their nets and became fishers of men. (Matthew 4:18-22)

I can only assume Jesus chose them because of their love of fishing. Their determination to remain focused on their task even when their nets came back empty. The patience they showed while sitting in their boats for hours at a time. Jesus knew, because of the desire for fishing God gave them, they had the skills needed to be fishers of men.

Nehemiah was a cupbearer to the king of Persia and he loved overseeing construction. After learning about Jerusalem's plight, Nehemiah wept and asked God for favor with the king so he could return to the city to help rebuild it. Jerusalem was in ruins and the walls of the city were literally falling down and gave little protection to the Jews returning from exile. (Nehemiah 1-7)

With blessings from the king, Nehemiah left for Jerusalem with letters to provide him safe passage and the supplies he would need. After his inspection of the wall, he got to work organizing the men and rebuilt the wall in just 52 days. (Nehemiah 6:15)

God knew Nehemiah's heart. He gave him his love for the people of Jerusalem. God blessed Nehemiah with abilities to deal with all kinds of people from his close work with the king. God helped develop Nehemiah's organizational skills and gave him his drive to finish the job quickly. Nehemiah was the perfect person to oversee the construction of the walls of Jerusalem, and God knew it.

In Genesis we are told Abraham was a wealthy livestock owner. Considering the rugged terrain Abraham was given to work with, being a successful shepherd was not easy. Constantly having to fight off the threat from wild animals and having to move the herd from place to place to find water and food was a huge challenge for even the most experienced herdsman. But Abraham loved his animals and excelled at taking care of them.

At 75 years old, Abraham was told by God to leave his family and go to the land He would show him. God promised Abraham He would make his people into a great nation and all the people on earth would be blessed through him. Abraham, his wife Sarah, and his nephew Lot left immediately for the Promised Land.

Can you imagine the faith it took for Abraham to leave his family – something rarely done at that time – and set out for the Promised Land? To believe he could father a nation when he and his wife Sarah had never been able to have a child? When Abraham was told by God nations would come from a son he and Sarah would have, Abraham and Sarah laughed out loud. "How can we have a child at our age," they thought. But they trusted God and He did what He said He would do and they had a son named Isaac. Just as God promised, with the birth of Isaac Abraham became the father of many nations. One of the nations would eventually include the birth of Jesus Christ.

Why do you think God chose Abraham to be the father of many nations? He was an old man in the twilight years of his life. Sarah, his wife, was childless and was way past her childbearing years. Because of Abraham's great faith and the abilities

God gave him as a shepherd, he had the skills needed to shepherd the people of many nations. Abraham's love of his livestock and his willingness to follow God made him the perfect candidate.

Simon Peter, Andrew, James, John, Nehemiah, and Abraham had all been given – from God – things they loved, things they liked to do. You are no different! What do you love? What do you like to do? Just like these great men, God gave you likes and dislikes for a reason. I pray you will spend quality time prayerfully exploring your likes and dislikes to determine why God gave them to you.

Through My Gifts, Special Talents, & Skills

Another way to help us discover what God created us to do is by examining our God-given gifts, special talents, and skills. Just as we have passions, likes and dislikes, God also gives us gifts and special talents to develop into skills to be used for our life's purpose, His plan for our lives. The Bible says in 1 Peter 4:10, *"Each of you should use whatever gift you have received to serve others, as faithful stewards of God's grace in its various forms."*

64

What are the gifts, special talents, and skills I'm talking about? For clarity, let's define all three. According to Encarta Dictionary:

A **gift** is a natural ability someone is born with – a God-given gift.

A **talent** is a gift which is developed through training and preparation.

A **skill** is the ability to do something well which is gained through experience over time.

Working together, our gifts, special talents, and skills complement our passions, likes and dislikes, and support our reason for living.

Here's how they work together: using our God-given gifts, we develop special talents with training and preparation. Over time, our special talents mature into skills which are used to fulfill our life's purpose. For example, let's say you have a God-given gift for music. You have good rhythm, pitch, and coordination. Because of your gift, you pursue playing the piano, singing, and dancing. With a little instruction and training, you realize you have a special talent for singing and decide to concentrate your time and effort on this one activity. With many years of preparation and practice, you develop into a highly skilled singer. Using your God-given gift of music, you develop a special talent for singing, and over time, a skill which is used to fulfill your reason for living.

We've all seen these gifts, special talents, and skills in others. For example, we all recognize the gift Tom Hanks has for acting. A two-time Academy Award winner, a four-time Golden Globe winner, a six-time Primetime Emmy® award winner, and with other awards too numerous to mention, it is easy for us to see his gift for learning and remembering lines, his special talent to make a script come alive, and his skill of transforming himself into a character we all can relate to.[3] Using his gifts, he perfected his special talents into skills which over time made him one of the best actors in Hollywood.

We all recognize the talent Peyton Manning has as a National Football League (NFL) quarterback. A first round draft pick in 1998, a five-time Most Valuable Player, named to 14 Pro Bowls, and with two Super Bowl Championships under his belt, it is easy for us to see his incredible eye-hand coordination, his special talent to read the defense and call the right play, and his skill to pass the ball with precision down the field.[4] Like Tom Hanks,

Peyton Manning used his gifts to perfect his special talents into skills which over time made him one of the best quarterbacks in history.

We all recognize the gift Elvis Presley had for singing.[5] With over a billion records sold worldwide, 150 different albums and singles which have been certified gold, platinum, or multiplatinum by the Recording Industry Association of America, and 18 singles which went to number one for a total of 80 weeks, it is easy for us to see his gift of vocal control, his special talent to write a catchy tune, and his skill to create an emotional attachment with the listener. Elvis used his gifts to perfect his special talents into skills which eventually made him the King of Rock and Roll.[6]

Unfortunately, unless our gifts are obvious we sometimes have trouble recognizing them. Oh it's easy for us to see the gifts of people like Tom Hanks, Peyton Manning, and Elvis Presley, but for some reason we tend to downplay our own God-given gifts when compared to those we so easily recognize in others.

Why do we have so much trouble recognizing and embracing our own gifts? Is it because our gifts are not as special or important as the gifts

God gives to others? Of course not! Every gift from God is special and important and is intended to give each of us the tools we need to be successful pursuing our life's purpose. The Bible says in James 1:17, *"Every good and perfect gift is from above, coming down from the Father of the heavenly lights, who does not change like shifting shadows."* However, when our gifts are not hit me between the eyes with a two-by-four obvious, we have to stop and listen to what God is telling us through our DNA.

To get you started, prayerfully answer these questions: What activities come easily to you? What are you good at with little effort? What comes naturally to you? What do other people say you're good at? If you won first prize at the county fair, what would it be for? What kinds of things do your friends come to you for when they need help? What special education or training do you have? What do you see as your strengths? Answers to these questions can provide valuable insight into your life and help you determine what God intended for you to do.

In 1 Kings we are told King Solomon had the gift of wisdom. In fact, after he became the king of Israel at 17, he sought God's help. God came to him in a dream and offered King Solomon any-thing he wanted. Unsure of his abilities to carry out his duties as King, Solomon asked the Lord for a discerning heart to govern his people and to be able to distinguish between right and wrong. Impressed with King Solomon's request, not only did God give King Solomon wisdom, He gave him riches and honor beyond any king of that time.

King Solomon best demonstrated his gift of wisdom when he determined the identity of the mother of a newborn baby. As the story goes, two women living in the same household had babies three days apart. During the night one of the women accidently rolled over on top of one of the babies and killed it. The remaining child was claimed by both women as the child's mother. King Solomon resolved the dispute by suggesting the baby be cut in half with a sword, giving one-half of the baby to each woman. One woman showed indifference to the King's suggestion. However, the other mother pleaded to King Solomon not to cut the baby in half, revealing her compassion for the child and the true mother of the baby. Because of the way King Solomon handled this situation, the kingdom of

Israel was in awe. Using his God-given gift, King Solomon developed his special talent of a discerning heart, the skill needed to understand what to do in difficult situations, and ruled the kingdom of Israel with an even hand.

In 1 Samuel 17 we are told David had the gift of courage. His courage became known to Israel when the forces of the Philistines and Israelites assembled for battle in the Valley of Elah. For 40 days a Philistine named Goliath taunted the Israelites and dared them to send a man out of their ranks to fight him. For 40 days the Israelites cowered and stayed in their battle lines afraid to send someone out to fight this giant of a man who stood over 9 feet tall.

David was only a young boy who tended to the family's few sheep. While visiting his brothers to bring them food, David heard about the challenge Goliath had proposed and he volunteered to fight the giant. After much discussion, King Saul agreed to David's request.

Armed with only five smooth stones and a sling, David made his way toward Goliath. Seeing David was only a boy, Goliath laughed and told him he would kill David and feed his flesh to the birds. But David wasn't afraid of Goliath like the other Israelites. He told Goliath this battle was the Lord's and he would kill him and cut his head off letting everyone know there is a God in Israel. As Goliath moved forward to begin his attack, David broke into a run and pulled a rock out of his bag, and with one swing of his sling, hit the Philistine in the forehead striking him dead. Just as David promised, he cut Goliath's head off using the Philistine's own sword and held it up for all the Israelites to see. Upon this action, the remaining Philistines turned and ran away.

How can a small boy overpower and kill a giant Philistine over 9 feet tall with only a sling? David was given the gift of courage from God. David took his gift and over time developed a special talent with his sling to fight off the many wild animals who tried to eat his family's sheep. Facing Goliath, he used the skill he developed with a sling to defeat the Philistine.

In Judges 13-16 we are told Samson had the gift of supernatural strength and was set apart by God for special service. But unlike King Solomon and David, his God-given gift was never developed to its full potential. Prepared by God to protect Israel from the Philistines, Samson was led by sin, instead of God. Samson had a passion for women, especially a Philistine woman named Delilah.

In the end, Delilah sold Samson out by giving away the secret of his strength. As soon as Delilah cut the hair Samson was never to shave, he was captured, blinded, and forced to grind grain for his enemies in prison.

Although Samson did finally return to God at the end of his life and gave some relief to the Israelites by destroying the temple of the Philistine god Dagon, he never became what he was created by God to become. Instead of leaning on God to direct his incredible strength to do the things he was created to do, Samson turned away from God and depended on himself and died in disgrace. Samson had unlimited potential because of the strength God gave him, but he fell short of his designed purpose, his reason for living.

Just like Tom Hanks, Peyton Manning, Elvis Presley, King Solomon, David, and Samson, we all have God-given gifts which are intended to be developed into special talents and skills important to God's plan in the world. Some of us recognize and easily develop our God-given abilities. However, most of us have to spend time praying and searching for what God created us to do. In the end, it comes down to one question: Who is going to control our gifts, special talents, and skills? Are we going to turn them over to God and let Him control our destiny and reap the rewards and joy He planned for us, or are we going to exclude God from our plans and use our God-given tools for our own purpose? If we decide to go on our own, we must remember, we will never live the incredible lives we were created by God to live. Like Samson, we will never have the success or joy we were intended to have. More often than not, our lives will be filled with disappointment and regret. The choice is ours.

What are your God-given gifts? What tools and abilities did God give you to develop into special talents and skills to fulfill your life's purpose? Seek God's leadership in all things and your gifts, special talents, and skills will be used to glorify God and fulfill His plan – your reason for living – in the world.

Through My Family Tree

Another way we determine what God created us to do is through our family tree. I believe God has purposely placed each of us into a family gene pool with the gifts, special talents, skills, and passions necessary to carry out our reason for living in the world. God has deliberately grouped us together with other people like us who inherit, carry, and pass along the same DNA from generation to generation.

Every family has a multitude of passions, gifts, and special talents which are shared by family members. It is up to each person to determine what God has specifically planned for them to do using the tools He's included in their family's DNA. Will every family member have the same gifts? No. Will every relative have the same talents or skills? Definitely not! Will every member of a family be passionate about the same things or have the same life purpose? Of course not! However, many do.

For example, many well-known families have shared the same God-given gifts, special talents, and passions throughout history. In politics we have the Bush family of George W., George H. W., Jeb, and the family patriarch Prescott Bush. The Kennedy family has John F., Robert F., Ted, Patrick, and Joe to name a few.[7] If nothing else, history has shown us there is something in their family gene pool which makes them passionate about public service.

In sports, we have the Manning family. Archie, Peyton, and Eli who were all exceptional football quarterbacks in college and the pros. In hockey, we have the Sutter family of Brian, Daryl, Duane, Rich, Ron, Brent, Brandon, and Brett. We also have the Howe family of Gordie, Mark, Marty, and Vic. In basketball we have the Rivers family of Doc, Uncle Jim Brewer, Cousins Ken Singleton and Byron Irvin, and children Austin, Jeremiah, and Callie.[8] All these families have shown their passions, gifts, and special talents for a particular sport throughout their family trees.

In entertainment, we have the Coppola family of Frances, Carmine, Sofia, Talia, Jason Schwartzman, and Nicholas Kim Coppola – better known as Nicolas Cage. We have the Huston family of Walter, Walter senior, Anjelica, John, and Danny. We have the Barrymore family of John, Ethel, Lionel, Georgie, John Drew, Diana, and perhaps the most famous of our generation, Drew Barrymore.[9] History has shown us these families have a passion for the entertainment industry and use their gifts and special talents to support their passions.

But a family doesn't have to be well-known or famous for its family members to share the same passions, gifts, or special talents. For example, in my family we have at least three generations who were trained as accountants, who spent years learning the profession, and developing the skills related to tracking the income and expenses of a business. It's obvious, even to an untrained eye, my family's DNA is programmed with a love of numbers and how they relate to running a successful organization.

In my wife's family, almost every discipline of engineering is represented. Civil, electrical, mechanical, and aerospace – just to name a few – are distributed throughout her family tree. These people have a love of math, critical thinking, and have spent many years learning how to apply their knowledge to real world problems. This passion to explore the unknown and to develop and design creative solutions is programmed into their DNA and helps define their reason for living.

What about your family? Do you have any family members who share the same occupation? Why did they choose their career path? What passions, gifts, and special talents do they share? Do you recognize any family members who have gone down different paths in life but still share the same passions, gifts, or special talents? What drives them? What caused them to take the life path they took?

How do you see your role or position in your family tree? Are you a patriarch, a leader, or do you relate more to another role within your family? Which of your family members are more like you? What are the passions, gifts, and special talents of the people you more closely identify with? What are their occupations? What characteristics propelled them into their family role? Do you share any of these same characteristics? Why do you relate to these family members? Understanding what drives other family members who share the same DNA you do may give you important insights into your own undiscovered passions, gifts, and special talents, which could ultimately lead you to what God created you to do.

Is it a coincidence our family members sometimes share the same passions, gifts, or special talents? I don't think so. Nor do I think a freak, random act of nature led this many family members down a similar life path. God has shown us throughout history He gives people within our family trees certain traits, passions, gifts, and special talents which are then passed from one generation to the next through our DNA to perpetuate the skills needed for our family's survival. Every cell in our bodies is perfectly designed as part of God's grand plan to fulfill our God-given purpose – our reason for living.

What are the passions, gifts, and special talents programmed into the genes of your family tree? What was your family designed to do in God's grand plan? What is your specific role? What are the God-given tools shared by family members within your tree? Who are the people in your family you relate to, who possibly share the same gifts, special talents, and drive you do? Thoroughly investigating your family tree could bring you a wealth of knowledge about what you were specifically created to do and give you clear direction about your life's purpose. I pray you will take time to talk to other family members to see what drives them and determine the gifts and passions they use to fulfill their God-given purpose. The insight you glean from your family may hold the clues you need to understand your life's purpose, your reason for living.

Through My Life-Changing Experiences

Sometimes it takes a life-changing experience to fully understand why God programmed us the way He did. It takes a "two-by-four" moment – good or bad – to help us fully understand our reason for living. For example, every time I go to Disney World it is a life-changing experience for me. In fact, when it is time to go home and I have to look over my shoulder and smell the pixie dust for the last time, I get very emotional. It's not that I don't want to go home, but Disney World holds a special place in my heart, and I'm never ready to leave.

My passion for Disney World started on my first trip in the 80s. For me, it is a magical place which conjures up happy memories spent with family and friends. It's a place that allows me time to get away from the hustle and bustle of life, recharge my batteries, and refocus on the important things in my life. On my first visit to Disney World I was so deeply moved by the experience, it set my life on a different path. Even to this day, I have a glass

souvenir I bought on my first trip that sits promi-
nently in my office displaying these words: "What
you dare to dream, dare to do!" Walt Disney's
words still motivate me today.

We've all had Disney type experiences
which affected us deeply. We've had incredible life-changing experiences which opened our
minds and eyes to possibilities never seen before.
We've had positive experiences which changed
our lives and gave our lives new direction, purpose, and meaning.

Unfortunately, not all life experiences are good,
and just like the good, bad experiences can be just
as life-changing. For example, it could be a death
in the family. It could be the loss of a job. It could
be an illness which affects the entire family. It
could be a tragedy which changes how we look or
think about things forever. It could be a divorce.
It could be an addiction to drugs or alcohol. In
short, it could be anything which creates a negative
life-changing experience.

Do you ever feel like you sometimes take two
steps forward and one step backward? Do you have
times when everything is going well and then
something happens and it knocks you down? Does

the pain you sometimes feel overwhelm you and cause your life to spin out of control? You're not alone. We all have these types of experiences, and sometimes they are more powerful and have a longer lasting effect on our lives than our Disney type experiences.

Let's face it; the world we live in is filled with pain. If you don't believe me, turn to any news channel on the television and watch it for five minutes. Stories of death and destruction dominate the headlines every day.

The pain we see on TV is only the tip of the iceberg. There is so much more pain in the world which never reaches the public eye. There are people struggling with an illness with little hope of recovery. There are people who have lost their job and may only be days away from becoming homeless. There are people who have lost hope and are besieged with thoughts of suicide.

As isolated as the bad times may make us feel, we are never alone. God is always with us, during the good times and especially during the bad. The Bible says in Matthew 28:20, *"And surely I am with you always, to the very end of the age."* God is with us to help us through our life-changing experiences and to share knowledge with us about His plan for our lives. If we listen closely, these experiences can provide clues about our reason for living and give direction concerning God's plan for our lives.

I believe the life-changing experiences we go through are a part of God's overall plan. They're a wake-up call. It's God's way of reminding us there are more important things in life than the many things that sometimes occupy and control our lives. By allowing these events to happen, God forces us to take time out of our busy lives to reflect on the paths our lives are taking. In essence, He permits a temporary pause in our daily routine to provide us an opportunity to evaluate our lives and make changes where necessary. Although these experiences can be painful, they are essential to our growth.

While bad life experiences may make us feel alone and cause us to consider giving up, we shouldn't. The Bible says in 2 Corinthians 4:16-18 (MSG)," *So we're not giving up. How could we! Even though on the outside it often looks like things are falling apart on us, on the inside, where God is making new life, not a day goes by without his unfolding grace. These hard times are small potatoes compared to the coming good times, the lavish celebration prepared for us. There's far more here than meets the eye. The things we see now are here today, gone tomorrow. But the things we can't see now will last forever."* Although sometimes our lives seem to be falling apart, they're not. God is creating a new person inside of us and preparing us for our life's purpose, and for things which will last forever.

How do we push through the bad times and stay focused on the bigger prize which awaits us? Here is a great thing about God's creation: God created our world with cycles to minimize our bad times. For example, the Earth rotates on a 24 hour cycle. The Earth circles the Sun every 365 days. The weeks of a month cycle every seven days. Everything in the universe works on a predefined cycle. Life experiences are the same. They also work through cycles. Some days are good while others are bad, but the bad days never last forever. Like all cycles in the universe which fight to find balance, good days are never far away. The Bible assures us in 1 Peter 5:10 (ERV), *"Yes, you will suffer for a short time. But after that, God will make everything right.*

He will make you strong. He will support you and keep you from falling. He is the God who gives all grace. He chose you to share in his glory in Christ. That glory will continue forever."

I think for us to get through the difficult times and learn the valuable lessons intended for our growth, we must do three things. First, we must rejoice in the bad times as well as the good. The Bible says in Romans 5:3-5 (Phillips), *"This doesn't mean, of course, that we have only a hope of future joys – we can be full of joy here and now even in our trials and troubles. Taken in the right spirit these very things will give us patient endurance; this in turn will develop a mature character, and a character of this sort produces a steady hope, a hope that will never disappoint us."* Bad times are designed to build our character and give us hope for the future. Just like good times, difficult times are part of the universal cycle and they can't be avoided. They are allowed by God for a reason and we must learn everything we can from them. When we endure the bad times, they make us stronger and prepare us for future days ahead.

Second, we must turn to God for direction in the good times as well as the bad. We must thank God for the good life-changing experiences and use these times to praise Him and give Him all the glory. During the bad times we must be patient, not get discouraged, and ask God to give us insight about our future and how this life-changing moment prepares us for our reason for living. We must comfort ourselves with the fact better days are coming and draw strength from the Lord. The Bible says in Nahum 1:7, *"The Lord is good, a refuge in times of trouble. He cares for those who trust in him."*

Finally, we must endure and overcome the difficult times. We must stand steadfast and never give up. We must stand strong in Christ and never allow the bad times to lessen our hope about our future. The apostle Paul told us in 2 Corinthians 12:10, *"That is why, for Christ's sake, I delight in weaknesses, in insults, in hardships, in persecutions, in difficulties. For when I am weak, then I am strong."* Why must we stay strong? Because the best God has to offer is yet to come.

Some of you are in pain today. A life-changing experience is controlling your every thought. Only God truly knows what you're going through. Although the world may seem like it is collapsing around you, I assure you it's not. While your mind may be dominated by the pain you're feeling right now, trust God and be assured that better days are coming. Be at peace, knowing God is in control. In John 16:33 Jesus said, *"I have told you these things, so that in me you may have peace. In this world you will have trouble. But take heart! I have overcome the world."*

I truly believe with all my heart every life-changing experience – good and bad – happens for a reason to support a bigger plan God has for each of us. Try to accept every life-changing experience as a teachable moment. By allowing them to happen to us, I think God is not only teaching us things to prepare us for our future tasks or responsibilities, He is making us dependent upon Him. Instead of being upset about why God has allowed something to happen to us, we should trust God and try to understand what He is wanting us to learn. During the times when we feel overburdened with life's lessons, take comfort in the fact the burdens we carry now are preparing us for greater rewards in the future. Pray to God to use your life-changing experiences to give you insight about your reason for living.

Through My Weaknesses

Going through school, I was never very good at English. It wasn't very high on my priority list. To be honest, I never thought I would need to master the skills taught in English class. All I thought about was playing sports.

Because of my lack of interest in English, at best, I was a "C" average student. In fact, one of my teachers along the way told me my writing skills were so bad it was a good thing I didn't want to be a writer! You know, she was right. At the time, I had no interest in becoming an author.

In college, although I always tried to do my very best, my skills didn't improve much. I had several good English teachers who spent a lot of time with me trying to improve my writing, but for whatever reason, I just didn't seem to be on the same page with everyone else. When classmates read passages from their papers out loud, I was amazed at how easily their words flowed and painted a picture in my head. My papers never did. The only pictures my papers ever painted were from the numerous red marks and deductions for bad grammar. My papers were never offered to be read aloud. It was obvious that writing was not my thing, nor would it ever be. I just didn't have the gift.

The entrance exam into seminary confirmed my writing fears and crushed my soul. Although I knew my lack of writing skills would be a problem, I never thought it would be a determining factor in following God's call. I entered seminary on probation and was assigned to a no credit, remedial writing class with the understanding, that if I wanted to stay in seminary, I had to pass the class. I was so embarrassed and ashamed I couldn't tell my family and friends. Worse yet, I questioned my calling. Why would God call me to do something I was not good at?

Knowing the challenge I faced, I did the only thing I could do. I prayed to God daily to help me get through the class. I knew I couldn't do it by myself. The only way I was going to stay in seminary was with God's help.

In hindsight, God had me just where he wanted me. If I was going to follow His call into the ministry and write books, I had to trust and follow Him. I had to be dependent on Him. God knew if He allowed me to only use my strengths, I would never turn to him and listen to His guidance, His plan for my life. I would do my own thing and depend on myself, not God. The Bible says in 1 Corinthians 1:27, *"But God chose the foolish things of the world to shame the wise; God chose the weak things of the world to shame the strong."*

We all have weaknesses, things we don't do so well. I believe God planted these things in our lives to force us to depend on Him to do the things He created us to do. God knew this when He designed us and He uses our weaknesses to show His strength to the world through us. As Paul told the church in Corinth in 2 Corinthians 12:7-9, *"Therefore, in order to keep me from becoming conceited, I was given a thorn in my flesh, a messenger of Satan, to torment me. Three times I pleaded with the Lord to take it away from me. But he said to me, "My grace is sufficient for you, for my power is made perfect in weakness." Therefore I will boast all the more gladly about my weaknesses, so that Christ's power may rest on me."*

The Bible is full of people with weaknesses used for God's glory. Moses and John had bad tempers. Gideon who God called "mighty warrior" was a coward at heart. Peter was impulsive, yet became "the rock." Abraham, who was faithful, twice said his wife was his sister so he wouldn't be killed. David was an adulterer, yet he became a man after God's own heart and followed his every commandment.

In case you are wondering, I passed the remedial writing class. I would like to tell you the class was easy and I aced it, but I didn't. It was one of the most difficult and stressful classes I have ever taken. God taught me an important lesson about how He uses our weaknesses to make us depend on Him. It was only through God's grace I received a "B" and was taken off probation. Even today, He continues to keep me humble and looking for His direction every time I sit down at the computer to write. He will use your weaknesses too, if you will trust Him. Pray to God He will highlight your weaknesses to give you strength as you pursue your God-given purpose.

***

So what have we learned? When we don't know or understand our reason for living, finding what God wants us to do is a multistep process. We have to look at our DNA – God's code – and appreciate how it is organized and the role it plays in our lives. As God designed it, the chromosomes, genes, and genetic switches work together to control our DNA and determine who we are and the traits we have. Recognizing the characteristics of our DNA is vital to helping us determine what God created us to do, setting the direction our lives were intended to travel, and finding the real joy God wants us to have.

Besides recognizing the characteristics of our DNA, we must also understand the passions God has given us and how they are meant to give us direction about our God-given purpose. For some of us, we know what drives us from the moment we are born. There has never been a question about what we are supposed to do with our lives. For others, our passion is not as obvious and we struggle to understand what we were created by God to do.

When we are unclear about our path, we must prayerfully examine all the clues God has given us through our DNA to support our drive and our purpose. How do we inspect the clues? We look closely at our likes and dislikes, gifts, special talents, skills, family tree, life-changing experiences, and weaknesses. When prayerfully examined together, these things give us a good indication of what God intended for us to do with our lives.

Once we understand and focus on our God-given purpose, our real life begins.

Endnotes

---

[1] Internet Movie Database (IMDB), "Mary Poppins (1964) Full Cast & Crew," imbd.com, Amazon, http://www.imdb. com/title/tt0058331/fullcredits/

[2] SongLyrics, "Mary Poppins – Pavement Artist (Chim Chim Cher-Ee) Lyrics," songlyrics.com, SongLyrics, http:// www.songlyrics.com/mary-poppins/pavement-artist-chim-chim-cher-ee-lyrics/

[3] Internet Movie Database (IMDB), "Tom Hanks Awards," imdb.com, Amazon, http://www.imdb.com/name/ nm0000158/awards

[4] Wikipedia, "Peyton Manning," Wikipedia.org, Wikipedia Foundation, Inc., http://en.Wikipedia.org/wiki/Peyton_ Manning

[5] The Estate of Elvis Presley, LLC, "Elvis," elvis.com, The Estate of Elvis Presley, LLC, http://www.elvis.com/

[6] Wikipedia, "Elvis Presley," Wikipedia.org, Wikipedia Foundation, Inc., http://en.Wikipedia.org/wiki/Elvis_Presley

[7] Aaron Blake and Sean Sullivan, "The biggest political dynasty in all 50 states," washingtonpost.com, The Washington Post, http://www.washingtonpost.com/blogs/the-fix/ wp/2012/10/05/the-biggest-political-dynasty-in-all-50-states/

[8] Podizz, "The Most Athletic Families of All Time," listology.com, Listology, http://www.listology.com/podizz/list/ most-athletic-families-all-time

[9] Orrin Konheim, "Top 10 Hollywood Family Dynasties," toptenz.net, TopTenz, http://www.toptenz.net/top-10-Hollywood-dynasties.php

6

What Is My Role In God's Plan?

When we become a child of God, whether we realized it at the time or not, we become a disciple of Jesus Christ. Encarta Dictionary defines a disciple as someone who believes in and follows the teachings of a leader, philosophy, or religion. Jesus said in Matthew 4:19, *"Come, follow me."* When we become a child of God and Jesus asks us to follow Him, it isn't a casual request someone makes in passing. It's not like a friend asking us to go with them to the grocery store to pick up a loaf of bread. When Jesus asks us to come follow Him, it becomes our reason for living. We become an integral part of God's overall plan.

Jesus describes our commitment to Him by painting a vivid three part picture of what's required of a disciple. In Matthew 16:24-26 Jesus said, *"Whoever wants to be my disciple must deny themselves and take up their cross and follow me."* Jesus makes it clear, if we want to be His disciple, we must first deny ourselves. We must deny our sinful nature. We must throw off our old self and put on the new. To deny one's self is to completely submit to the lordship of Jesus Christ.

Second, we are asked to take up our cross. Taking up our cross is a willingness to endure and accept the ridicule, harassment, rejection, and persecution which will surely follow us as a disciple of Jesus Christ. Jesus is warning us that being a disciple of His is not going to be easy. There are people who will make fun of us for believing in Him. There are people who will turn their backs on us and tell others they don't know us. There are people who will want to hurt us, mentally and physically. Being a disciple of Christ is not for the faint of heart.

The symbolism of the cross was well-known to the early disciples and the people of that time. The cross was used to torture and kill anyone who was an enemy of Rome. Anyone who dared to go against the authority of the government was nailed to the cross, suffering a horrible death. So when Jesus told them to take up their cross, the people knew exactly what He meant. He was preparing them for the suffering they would surely experience being His disciple.

Finally, as a disciple we are required to follow Him in loyal obedience. Once we deny ourselves and take up our cross, only then are we prepared to follow Jesus. We are to follow Him without question. We are to submit to His leadership in all things. We are to incorporate His teachings into our daily living and focus on Him for our direction.

Several years ago on our anniversary Mary made one of my dreams come true. She gave me a trip to the Richard Petty Driving Experience at Talladega Raceway. There's not a better place to experience the power of a racecar than at a superspeedway where cars routinely go over 200 mph.

Before letting any of us get behind the wheel of a racecar, my class went through four hours of hands-on training. We listened intently as the instructors described all the systems of the car and how they worked together. They explained the signals the flagman would use to give us information as we lapped the track. Once in the racecar, they insisted we never leave the car unless instructed to do so. They assured us, as long as we followed their instructions completely, we would be safe.

Next, they took us on a 110+ mph tour around the track in a 15 passenger van. Our professional driver sat sideways in the driver's seat with his left foot on the accelerator and his left hand on the steering wheel. As he talked to us over the back of his seat, he never looked through the windshield of the van as we raced around the track. At times we came within inches of the outside wall. I can't speak for my fellow classmates, but I was terrified.

When it was finally time to drive, I was understandably nervous. Even today I can still remember sitting behind the wheel of the racecar desperately trying to hang on to every word of training I had just received. All of the instructions raced through my head as I left the pit box headed for the racetrack. Although they guaranteed us the car we were driving was safer than our own car, fear gripped me as I considered the dangers I faced if I made a mistake and lost control of the car.

Just in front of my car was a professional driver in another racecar who would set my line and pace around the track. I was instructed to stay within two car lengths of his car at all times. He promised me that, if I maintained my line and distance correctly, each lap would be faster than the lap before. He insisted, "Bobby, even if I leave the track and go through the drive-thru at McDonald's, you are to follow me." I was to trust him completely and follow him without question wherever he went.

My turn finally came. As you might imagine, I followed the professional driver as I was instructed, never taking my eyes off his back bumper. Just as they had promised, each lap was faster than the last. My quickest lap timed out at over 155 mph, second fastest in my class. Never have I gone so fast or driven a car with so much power.

When we agree to follow Jesus Christ, like the professional driver I followed around the track at Talladega, Jesus becomes the professional driver of our lives. We are to follow Him without question. We are to keep our eyes focused on Jesus and let Him set our line and pace. When we do, just as we were promised to go faster each lap, Jesus rewards us with additional responsibilities. Great responsibility is given to those who completely trust the Lord!

However, there is more to our role in God's plan than becoming a disciple. Not only are we to follow Jesus wherever He leads us, He also wants us to become fishers of men. In Matthew 4:19 Jesus said, *"Come, follow me and I will send you out to fish for people."* He wants us to tell other people about Jesus so they can have the opportunity to become His disciples too.

To Become Fishers Of Men

In Matthew 28:19-20 the Great Commission tells us to "go *and make disciples of all nations, baptizing them in the name of the Father and of the Son and of the Holy Spirit, and teaching them to obey everything I have commanded you.* We are to tell everyone about Jesus. We are to tell everyone about His love and his desire for all people to follow Him.

As children of God, we sometimes get confused about the Great Commission. We convince ourselves Jesus' commandment doesn't speak directly to us. We incorrectly believe witnessing to people who don't know Jesus is reserved for the pastors, priests, and evangelists of the world, not us. We rationalize our directive is to only talk about Jesus and share His love with those who already love Him. And although sharing with other Christians is important to God's overall plan, when we neglect to share Jesus with non-Christians we ignore and exclude the rest of the population. We disregard the people who desperately need the love of Jesus in their lives.

In the early 80s my wife and I were members of a Baptist church in southern Kentucky. It was a prominent church in the community where almost everyone in our little town attended. When I say little town, I do mean little. The first week after moving there someone told us, "Chances are you will never be mugged in our little town, but if you are, you will know who did it." The town was so small everyone seemed to know everybody.

One hot, Sunday morning we had a visitor at church. She was an elderly lady who didn't move so well anymore. And although the town prided itself in knowing everyone who lived there, no one seemed to know the stranger who showed up that morning.

Sitting in the front row, the little lady stood out like a sore thumb. She was dressed in a heavy buttoned up red winter coat with imitation fur around the collar. Her hair, although recently combed, didn't have any of the current hair styles of the day. Her shoes were worn but nicely kept. When the collection plate was passed, she emptied her change purse of a few coins which clinked in the plate.

At the end of the service did we follow Jesus' teachings and all rush to meet her and welcome her to our church? No. We – myself included – completely ignored her. We avoided her as if she had the plague. I mean, who in their right mind would wear a buttoned up heavy winter coat to church on a hot summer day? Based on her appearance, in our minds we concluded she didn't belong at our church and we made no attempt to reach out to her. We never saw her again.

We – I – failed as a disciple of Jesus Christ that day. She didn't fit the mold I had erroneously created in my head of who I was commissioned to disciple. As a result, I excluded her. I turned my back on her. I failed God. Although God has forgiven me, I still regret not reaching out to her, some 30 years later. In Mark 2:17 Jesus said, *"It is not the healthy who need a doctor, but the sick. I have not come to call the righteous, but sinners."* As a follower of Jesus Christ we are instructed to witness to all people of all nations, races, and creeds – even little ladies wearing a buttoned up red winter coat on a hot summer day.

The best way to tell others about Jesus is by sharing what God has done in our lives. In Acts 1:8 Jesus said, *"You will be my witnesses in Jerusalem, and in all Judea and Samaria, and to the ends of the earth."* Just like a witness in a courtroom, we are to testify and tell people what God has done for us and how His love has transformed us into the person we are today.[1] I think Paul said it best to the Ephesian elders in Acts 20:24, *"I consider my life worth nothing to me; my only aim is to finish the race and complete the task the Lord Jesus has given me—the task of testifying to the good news of God's grace."*

When we become a child of God, we receive the Holy Spirit and it instantly becomes our purpose to become a disciple of Christ. We are commanded to deny ourselves, take up our cross, and follow Him. We are instructed to tell all people about God's grace, His word, and His love. It's not a choice, but our reason for living. No rock is to be left unturned. No person is to be left behind. All people deserve the grace of God and His transforming presence in their lives. God has picked each of us for a special purpose in order to share His love with the world.

As a disciple of Christ sharing the love of God with others, we are also commanded to become more Christlike.

To Become More Christlike

Words cannot adequately describe my conversion experience when I became a child of God. In hindsight, I guess more than anything else it was an intense feeling which surrounded me at the nightly campfire service. A feeling which seemed as if the weight of the world was being lifted from my shoulders, a heavy load I didn't realize I was carrying. My heart filled with love – God's love – and a joy came over me like I had never felt before. When I asked Jesus into my heart, the emptiness and aloneness I felt instantly went away and I felt a presence – God's presence – embracing me. It was as if God himself was hugging me.

I'm sure you know the feeling I'm talking about. Remember the feeling when one of your parents hugged you as a child to comfort you and tell you everything was going to be all right? A hug beyond all human understanding which let you immediately know they loved you unconditionally and were there for you always. This was the feeling I felt.

My most memorable parent hug came from my father when I was 20 years old. I was taking 16 credit hours at my local college in the daytime and working 40 plus hours a week at a box manufacturing company at night. I was so busy working and going to school I only averaged around two hours of sleep per night. Why did I keep this crazy schedule? I was in love. I felt it was necessary to burn the candle at both ends in order to create a solid foundation for Mary and me to get married.

Although working full time and carrying a full load at college kept me both mentally and physically exhausted, it had its benefits. I was able to purchase my first new car, something I desperately needed. It was a beautiful little red car. It got great gas mileage, much different from the gas guzzler I had before.

Unfortunately, only a month into my new car experience, I had a serious wreck while driving from school to work one afternoon. My new car was completely destroyed. It didn't even have 1,000 miles on the odometer. Worse yet, the accident injured several people in the other car. The accident was my fault and I was devastated.

Lying in bed, all I could think about was how the accident was going to affect Mary and my plans to get married. To be honest, with the litigation and the expenses which were sure to come as the result of the wreck, in my mind, our future seemed to be slipping away. Overwhelmed with emotion, I laid in my bed staring at the ceiling of my bedroom not knowing what to do.

Seeing how upset I was, my dad came into my room and sat on the floor by my bed. He began to cry with me. I had never seen my dad cry before. After a short time, he stood up and draped his body over mine and began to hug me and assure me everything was going to be all right. He seemed to know just the right things to say as we laid there for hours talking. It was the best hug my dad ever gave me.

Although the compassion he showed me was amazing and came at just the right moment, it is not the reason his hug was so memorable. You see, my dad was not a touchy, feely kind of guy. Although he was a very loving dad, he rarely expressed his feelings with physical contact. I don't know if it was because of the era he grew up in or what, but that's who he was. However, this time for whatever reason, he was different. He stepped outside of his comfort zone and hugged me like never before. His physical presence assured me everything was going to be OK. His fatherly hug gave me hope and courage to face the next day.

When we become children of God, our heavenly Father – just like our earthly father – comes to us wherever we are and embraces us with His compassion and love and assures us everything is going to be all right. He promises to be with us always – in the good times and bad – to comfort us and give us direction through whatever we are facing.

How does God make his presence known to us? He makes His presence known to us through the Holy Spirit. When we become a child of God, we receive the Holy Spirit and the Spirit of God lives within us. It's through the Holy Spirit God hugs and comforts us and gives us direction. Scripture tells us in Romans 15:13, *"May the God of hope fill you with all joy and peace as you trust in him, so that you may overflow with hope by the power of the Holy Spirit."*

Besides comforting us, one of the major roles of the Holy Spirit is to change our lives and make us more Christlike. God wants His children to grow up, mature, and have the characteristics of Jesus Christ. The Bible says in Ephesians 4:14-15, *"Then we will no longer be infants, tossed back and forth by the waves, and blown here and there by every wind of teaching and by the cunning and craftiness of people in their deceitful scheming. Instead, speaking the truth in love, we will grow to become in every respect the mature body of him who is the head, that is, Christ."*

Unfortunately, spiritual growth doesn't happen overnight. Just as a newborn baby doesn't walk or talk from the moment he or she is born, spiritual growth through the Holy Spirit doesn't happen immediately. It takes time to grow and mature and develop the skills necessary to become a mature Christian. Like a newborn baby, spiritual growth happens through gradual changes.

Why does it take time to become a mature Christian? When we become a child of God we still have all the bad habits, attitudes, and thoughts from our former life fighting against our desire to become more like Christ. And, as we all know from personal experience, good habits, attitudes, and more appropriate thoughts take time to develop. It doesn't happen overnight. Our new self is constantly battling with our old self for control. But that's OK. You see, quick changes typically don't last very long anyway. Not until we've had time for our new habits, attitudes, and thoughts to become part of our instinctive muscle memory, will the changes become permanent. The only way this can happen is for our new skills to be practiced over and over again until they become part of our normal behavioral pattern. This takes time. The Bible says in Hebrews 5:13-14, *"Anyone who lives on milk, being still an infant, is not acquainted with the teaching about righteousness. But solid food is for the mature, who by constant use have trained themselves to distinguish good from evil."*

Although God in His infinite power could instantly make us spiritually mature, He chooses to do it gradually, over time. God knows bad habits, attitudes, and thoughts are hard to change quickly in a lasting way. For this reason, He chooses to do it the right way, slowly developing muscle memory which will stand the test of time. The scriptures tell us in James 1:4, we are to *"Let perseverance finish its work so that you may be mature and complete, not lacking anything."*

The kind of spiritual growth necessary to become Christlike starts in our mind. We must refocus our thoughts and completely submit to Jesus Christ. The Bible says in Romans 12:2, *"Do not conform to the pattern of this world, but be transformed by the renewing of your mind. Then you will be able to test and approve what God's will is—his good, pleasing and perfect will."* Using our minds, over time we must throw off the things of our old life – bad habits, attitudes, and thoughts – and put on our new selves with the help of the Holy Spirit to form our new life in Christ.

To throw off the things of our old life we must submit control of our minds to God and make the changes necessary to become Christlike through facing the truth revealed to us by the Holy Spirit. We are taught in Ephesians 4:21-23, *"when you heard about Christ and were taught in him in accordance with the truth that is in Jesus. You were taught, with regard to your former way of life, to put off your old self, which is being corrupted by its deceitful desires; to be made new in the attitude of your minds; and to put on the new self, created to be like God in true righteousness and holiness.*"

How do we know which things from our old life should be discarded as we develop our muscle memory and build our new life? We build our new life through the truth in God's Holy Word. The Bible says in 2 Timothy 3:16-17, "*All Scripture is God-breathed and is useful for teaching, rebuking, correcting and training in righteousness, so that the servant of God may be thoroughly equipped for every good work.*" Not until we confront the things which control our lives with the truth the Holy Spirit provides us through God's word can we make the changes needed to become like Jesus. Simply stated, not until we give control of our minds to God and confront our bad habits, attitudes, and thoughts with the help of the Holy Spirt and the truth that comes from God's word, can change – lasting change – take place.

This confrontation of the truth in our lives happens through repentance. A good rule of thumb to follow when seeking the truth and confronting the things of our lives which need changing can be found in James 3:17. "*The wisdom that comes from heaven is first of all pure; then peace loving, considerate, submissive, full of mercy and good fruit, impartial and sincere."* In other words, are our habits, attitudes, and thoughts pure? If they are not, they are not from God. Are our habits, attitudes, and thoughts peace-loving? If they promote conflict, they are not from God. Are our habits, attitudes, and thoughts considerate? If they are not understanding of others and their feelings, they are not from God. Are they submissive? If they are an unloving attempt to control what happens to us and/or events around us, they are not from God. Are they full of mercy and good fruit? If they do not show compassion, kindness, or forgiveness, they are not from God. Are they impartial and sincere? If our habits, attitudes, and thoughts are biased, favoring one person over another, or they are not honest, trying to hide the real meaning, they did not come from God.

So, what are the characteristics we are to fill our hearts with to make us more like Christ? They are described in the Bible in Galatians 5:22-23 as the fruits of the spirit. They are love, joy, peace, patience, kindness, goodness, faithfulness, gentleness, and self-control. The fruits of the spirit are the characteristics God wants us to exhibit in our lives. Demonstrating the fruits of the spirit in all our actions is an outward sign of a changed heart.

How do we exhibit our growth and maturity in Christ? We demonstrate our maturity in Christ by using the fruits of the spirit as our guiding light when dealing with, and helping others. The keywords to focus on here are the words "when helping others." Think about this: Is the fruit produced by a tree created to benefit the tree? Of course not! The fruit is used to bring nourishment to those who eat it. Likewise, the fruit produced through us with the help of the Holy Spirit is not to be used to feed us, but is to be used to nourish and help others.

When we begin to give control of our minds to God, face the truth with the help of the Holy Spirit, and depend on the word of God for understanding and direction, we begin to set our life's path on the Spirit rather than on the things of the world. And, when this happens, our fruit begins to grow, mature, and flourish, not to satisfy us, but to benefit others we were called to serve. Following the leadership of the Holy Spirit, we must deny our old selves, control our minds with the help of God's word, and serve others with the attitude produced through the fruit of the spirit. When we do, we become more Christlike.

Another role we have in God's plan is to love our neighbors as ourselves.

To Love Our Neighbors As Ourselves

When I hear this command I think of Matthew 7:12 and the Golden Rule: *"So in everything, do to others what you would have them do to you."*

How we treat others, most often, determines how they treat us. If we want people to treat us with respect, we must first treat them with respect. If we want people to listen to us, we must first listen to them. If we want people to love and care for us, we must first love and care for them.

But the Golden Rule only explains half of what is expected of a child of God. Sure, we must first treat others how we want to be treated, but being a follower of Jesus Christ goes much farther. We are to treat others as we want to be treated, even if they don't give us the same respect; even if they shun our attempts to love them or reject us completely. We are to love them no matter how they respond to us, even if they hate us. We are to love everyone as we love ourselves.

Why do we have to love someone who hates us? Why, because God is love. The entire basis of Jesus' existence is based on love. Think of it this way: Jesus is saying everything in the entire universe in the past, present, and future is based on love. The Bible says in 1 Corinthians 16:14, *"Do everything in love."* All God wants us to do is love Him and each other unconditionally.

Can you imagine how different the world would be if everyone loved God unconditionally and our neighbors as we love ourselves? All hate and war would be eliminated everywhere in the world. Mistrust and deception would go away. Theft and robbery would be eradicated. Hunger would be a thing of the past. Honestly, if everyone made "love God with all your heart and your neighbor as yourself" an integral part of his or her life, we would eliminate every type of evil in the world. Jesus must weep in heaven when He looks down upon us and sees the mess our world is in today.

Growing up in the 50s and 60s was much different than it is today. My parents never locked the doors of our home, even when we went on vacation.

On the rare occasion they did, they kept a spare key under the welcome mat just in case someone needed to open the door.

The key to our car was left in the ignition switch or over the sun visor. The key never went into my mom's or dad's pocket or came into the house. It stayed in the unlocked car in case someone needed it.

Considering how our world is today, it is hard to imagine anyone being so trusting of their fellow man. But people were different back then. People seemed more respectful of each other and never envisioned anyone breaking into their house or stealing their car.

So what happened? As a people, we have forgotten God's commandments. In some cases, we have purposely erased them from our minds and separated ourselves from God. The Bible says in 1 John 4:16, *"God is love. Whoever lives in love lives in God, and God in them."* When we don't live in love, God doesn't live in us. It is the absence of God's love which has created the world we live in today.

We are to love one another unconditionally as Jesus has unconditionally loved us. In John 15:12 Jesus said, *"My command is this: Love each other as I have loved you.*" God showed His love and commitment to us even before we were born. He willingly sacrificed His son Jesus, who freely gave His life on a cross for our sins. If God and Jesus can love us so completely, how can we not love our neighbors as Jesus has commanded us to love them? When we love one another, God lives in us and His love is made complete. (1 John 4-12)

What about my enemies? How can God expect me to love them? In Luke 6:27-31 Jesus said, "*To you who are listening I say: Love your enemies, do good to those who hate you, bless those who curse you, pray for those who mistreat you. If someone slaps you on one cheek, turn to them the other also. If someone takes your coat, do not withhold your shirt from them. Give to everyone who asks you, and if anyone takes what belongs to you, do not demand it back. Do to others as you would have them do to you.*" See the Golden Rule again? Loving unconditionally as Jesus loves us includes everyone, even our enemies.

Loving our enemies is the true test of our commitment to love our neighbors unconditionally. Anyone can love someone who loves them. Anyone can treat someone respectfully if they are respected. However, it takes the power of God's love to unconditionally love our enemies. The Bible says in Romans 15:7, *"Accept one another, then, just as Christ accepted you, in order to bring praise to God."* When we love everyone unconditionally – including our enemies – we praise God!

Now the love we're talking about here is much more than just saying we love someone. The love here is much more than words or a feeling. The love Jesus is talking about is revealed by our actions. The Bible says in 1 John 3:18, *"Dear children, let us not love with words or speech but with actions and in truth."* The apostle Paul describes the love Jesus is talking about to the Corinthians: *"Love is patient, love is kind. It does not envy, it does not boast, it is not proud. It does not dishonor others, it is not self-seeking, it is not easily angered, it keeps no record of wrongs. Love does not delight in evil but rejoices with the truth. It always protects, always trusts, always hopes, always perseveres. Love never fails."* (1 Corinthians 13:4-8)

The way Paul describes love is how God loves us. I love the way the New Living Translation® (NLT) describes it in 1 Corinthians 13:7: *"Love never gives up, never loses faith, is always hopeful, and endures through every circumstance."* This is how we are to love our neighbors. We are to believe in our neighbors and never give up on them, even when they disappoint us. We are to never lose faith or stop believing in them. We are to remain hopeful and optimistic our neighbors will do the right thing. Our love for our neighbors is to endure and withstand every circumstance faced. This is how God loves us and how we are to love others.

God is love. When we love God, He loves us. When we love our neighbors, God loves us. When we love our enemies, God loves us. When we love God and our neighbors unconditionally, God's love is made complete!

How do we love God and our neighbors unconditionally? We love them through our acts of service to God, the church, and the world.

To Serve God, The Church, And The World

When we were conceived in our mother's womb, God shaped and formed us with a purpose in mind. Using our DNA, He molded us with passions, gifts, and abilities to prepare us for the purpose He intended for us to accomplish. Even before our hearts started beating, God had a plan for us, a reason for our lives.

When we accept Jesus Christ as our Lord and Savior, we are given a new life. The Holy Spirit enters our bodies to prepare us for the good works God planned for us to live our lives doing. The Bible says in Ephesians 2:10, *"For we are God's handiwork, created in Christ Jesus to do good works, which God prepared in advance for us to do."*

How does the Holy Spirit prepare us for our purpose? When we submit to the Holy Spirit, He takes our God-given passions, gifts, and abilities and leads us down the path God intended for our lives to travel. Through this transformational process, the Holy Spirit gives us direction about how we are to serve God, the church, and the world in which we live. The Living Bible puts it this way, *"It is God himself who has made us what we are and given us new lives from Christ Jesus; and long ages ago he planned that we should spend these lives in helping others."* (Ephesians 2:10)

One of the gifts God has blessed me with may be considered a curse to most people. He has given me the ability to quickly understand the worst which can happen in any given situation. Instead of first looking at the most positive thing which may happen, I tend to look at the negative. Most people look at my gift as undesirable, a "half empty glass" approach to life.

However, I don't look at it this way at all. For over 25 years I was a disaster planner. I helped companies design strategies to prevent disasters from destroying their businesses. This God-given gift allowed me to quickly find the weaknesses in a company's strategy and help them develop plans which would keep their businesses running in the event of a catastrophe.

Although this God-given gift served me well as a disaster planner, God had a bigger plan for me. It was only through the leadership of the Holy Spirit that I realized the full potential of my gift. My gift was not only to be used to help organizations survive disasters, but God wanted me to use my gift to help others with their personal tragedies. As a result, throughout my life God has crossed my path with people who needed the comfort of my gift to help them understand and mitigate their personal problems.

To be honest, at first I considered the stream of people God sent my way a punishment. I was overwhelmed at the number of people who would seek me out and share the most private details of their lives. Many of these people, I didn't even know. I would be sitting somewhere and someone would sit down beside me and start sharing their problems with me. It scared me! Why would a complete stranger do this? Worse yet, I didn't feel qualified to solve their problems.

Over time, and with the help and direction of the Holy Spirit, I began to better understand the role I played in God's overall plan for my life. God uses my gift to help people through their personal disasters. At times my God-given gift is used to quickly get to the root of the problem and present possible alleviating solutions. Other times, God just wants me to listen. He wants me to listen with a loving ear and not be judgmental.

Without the direction of the Holy Spirit in my life, my God-given gift would have never been used for its intended purpose. It would have never been used to help others, to serve others, to love others. Only after we accept Jesus Christ as our Lord and Savior and follow the leadership of the Holy Spirit do we have the ability to use our God-given gifts to their full potential as God intended them to be used. God makes it clear we are to use our passions, gifts, and talents to serve Him, the church, and the world. Despite what you have been told or may believe, this is our real reason for living. This is what God created us to do!

How does God want us to serve Him? The answer is in Deuteronomy 10:12 (MSG): *"So now Israel, what do you think God expects from you? Just this: Live in his presence in holy reverence, follow the road he sets out for you, love him, serve God, your God, with everything you have in you, obey the commandments and regulations of God that I'm commanding you today— live a good life."* God wants us to love Him with all of our hearts, with all of our souls, and with all of our minds. He wants us to love our neighbors as ourselves. God wants us to always make Him first in our lives and follow His direction in all things. When we follow God's plan for our lives, He gives us our reason for living.

God really wants us to live a good life. He wants us to be happy and successful. Does this mean our lives will be free of trials and tribulations? Of course not! God never promised us a life free of problems or difficulties. However, only when we love God completely and follow His leadership in all things will we live the life God intended for us to live. The Bible says in Romans 8:28, *"And we know that in all things God works for the good of those who love him, who have been called according to his purpose."*

In addition to serving God, we are to use our passions, gifts, and talents to serve the church. Remember when we talked about how our God-given gifts develop into talents and skills? The church is where we develop our gifts into something we can use for the glory of God. Not only is it our place to serve other Christians, it is our safe place to grow and prepare for what God created us to accomplish in the world. In 1 Corinthians 12:7 (MSG) the Bible says, *"God's various gifts are handed out everywhere; but they all originate in God's Spirit. God's various ministries are carried out everywhere; but they all originate in God's Spirit. God's various expressions of power are in action everywhere; but God himself is behind it all. Each person is given something to do that shows who God is: Everyone gets in on it, everyone benefits."* The church is the body of Christ where each part – each person – perfects their gifts to serve the world.

Will the gifts we use to serve the church be the same gifts we use to serve the world? Not necessarily. We may be led to do something in the church we know nothing about, and that's OK. God puts us in places where He needs us. For example, maybe there is a person serving in a certain area of the church God needs us to befriend and counsel. Maybe there is a skill we need to learn to enhance the gifts we were given. Maybe the experience of serving in a particular area will give new meaning to our gifts and send us in a different direction. Whatever the reason, God has a reason for us to serve there. Therefore, we should always be open to where we are being led to serve in the church. The Bible says in Ephesians 4:16, "*From him the whole body, joined and held together by every supporting ligament, grows and builds itself up in love, as each part does its work.*" Wherever we are asked to serve, God has a plan and He needs our gifts to build the church.

Finally we are to use our passions, gifts, and talents to serve the world. The Bible says in 1 Peter 4:10, "*Each of you should use whatever gift you have received to serve others, as faithful stewards of God's grace in its various forms.*" As a disciple of Christ, we represent His body to the world. We are His hands, feet, and eyes, and play a role in God's plan for the world.

Paul addressed how we are to serve the world in his letter to the Corinthians, "*Each person should live as a believer in whatever situation the Lord has assigned to them, just as God has called them."* (1 Corinthians 7:17) According to Paul, we are to serve wherever God has led us to be. If we are a postman, we are to serve the world as a postal worker. If we are a mechanic, we are to serve others as we repair their cars. If we are an executive at a Fortune 500 company, we are to serve the world showing God's love to the company we oversee. Wherever we are serving, we are to serve the people of the world so they can see God's love in us and grow to love Him. When we serve others, we serve God at the same time.

Unfortunately, we live in a "me first" world which makes it difficult for us to put others before ourselves. We've been led to believe we deserve the best of everything. We're told that if we want to be first in life, we may have to step on a few people along the way to get there.

We weren't created this way. That's not how God designed us. God didn't say put yourself first. The world did. The world tries to change us by playing on our insecurities and by telling us God can't take care of us. The world tells us we control our future, not God. Don't believe it!

When you do something nice for someone doesn't it make you feel good about yourself? Sure it does! For a brief moment your whole body seems to smile, to do a little happy dance. Do you think this feeling is just a coincidence? Of course not; God designed you this way. When you help people and put their needs before yours, your body excretes endorphins into your bloodstream and makes you feel happy. It is God's physical confirmation to you that you are following His plan for your life.

I will never forget the inspirational news story several years ago when at a Special Olympics event one of the participants tripped and fell a few yards from the finish line. Instead of all the other runners looking over their shoulders and saying "sorry about your luck" like in a typical race, they stopped, went back, helped the fallen runner up, and they all crossed the finish line together. It didn't matter to them who won. What mattered was they all finished the race. We can all learn a lot from their unselfish act of love, putting the needs of someone else above their own.

We have been falsely led by the world to believe the only way to be truly happy is by pleasing ourselves first. We've been taught happiness comes from putting ourselves before everyone else and staying focused on our needs. In fact, the complete opposite is true. If we want to be truly happy, we must put the needs of others before ours. In total contrast to what the world wants us to believe, we must love others more than we love ourselves to find real happiness, the joy only God can provide.

How do we love others? We love others by using our God-given gifts, talents, and resources to love our neighbors as God loves us. Let us never forget everything we have comes from God. Our gifts come from God. Our talents come from God. Our time we have on earth comes from God. Our money comes from God. Everything we have now and everything we will have in the future is a gift from God. More importantly, God's gifts were given to us with the explicit purpose of serving others. The Bible says in Ephesians 2:10, *"For we are God's handiwork, created in Christ Jesus to do good works, which God prepared in advance for us to do."* The "good works" Paul is talking about in his letter to the Ephesians is serving our neighbors. We were created to serve others and complete the tasks God has given us to do.

When we serve our neighbors, we serve God. In Matthew 25:40 Jesus said, *"Truly I tell you, whatever you did for one of the least of these brothers and sisters of mine, you did for me."* For example, when we provide a meal to a homeless person, we serve God. When we console a friend after the death of a family member, we serve God. When we show kindness to a complete stranger, we serve God. Whenever we do anything for someone else through an act of love, we serve God and do what He created us to do. And when we put the needs of others before ours we are rewarded, not only with a quick burst of endorphins in our bloodstream, we are rewarded for eternity in heaven. The Bible says in Ephesians 6:7-8, *"Serve wholeheartedly, as if you were serving the Lord, not people, because you know that the Lord will reward each one for whatever good they do, whether they are slave or free."*

Simply put, whenever we serve others – our neighbors – using the gifts and resources God has given us to use, we not only serve God, we do what God created us to do. We find our reason for living. We find sustaining happiness, the joy only God can give.

When was the last time you felt good about doing something for someone else? When was the last time you put someone else's needs before your own? God created us for a reason – to serve others. Everything we have has been given to us so we may carry out God's plan in the world, our God-given purpose.

By loving and serving God we are given divine direction through the Holy Spirit and a reason for living. By serving the church we are given fellowship with other believers where we can develop our God-given gifts in a safe place and prepare for our mission in the world. By serving the world we fulfill the Great Commission using our gifts to lead people to Christ and build the body of believers. Serving God, serving the church, and serving the world is essential to fulfilling God's purpose for our lives. Serving God, the church, and the world is essential to doing what God created us to do.

---

[1] Rick Warren, "Tell Others Your Great God Story," rickwarren.org, Rick Warren, http://rickwarren.org/devotional/english/tell-others-your-great-god-story

7

What Happens When I Follow God's Plan For My Life?

When we turn our lives over to Jesus Christ, submit to the leadership of the Holy Spirit, and embrace the programming and tools God has given us through our gifts, likes and dislikes, passions, and family tree we find our reason for living. We discover what God created us to do!

Unfortunately, sometimes we let the noise of life get in the way of us staying focused on the path God wants us to follow. When this happens, I think God nudges us along our path by reminding us of a weakness we may have or by allowing a life experience – good or bad – to deeply move us. When I think back on my life, there have been many times when I thought God was prodding me along to help me keep my eyes on the path He planned for me to follow.

When everything works as God designed it, we find our reason for living and it is life changing. Instead of drifting aimlessly from day to day, from one thing to the next, we understand what is important and what isn't, and our priorities begin to focus. It's like a lightbulb goes off in our head and the path, that up until this point has been obscured in darkness, is illuminated and everything about our life comes into sharp focus. Our priorities stand out like the tallest trees in the forest.

My Priorities Focus

A priority, according to the *Encarta Dictionary*, means "the state of having the most importance or urgency, somebody or something ranked highly in terms of importance, and/or the right to be ranked above all others."[1] In short, a priority represents something which is most important to us. When it comes to God, our priorities are the things most important to doing what God created us to do.

There are three levels of priorities we must focus on to accomplish what God created us to do. First, we must remain focused on God. He is always our top priority. Our very existence comes from Him. Everything we have or will have is the direct result of His presence in our lives. He made us who we are and will direct us toward who we are to become. Without God we have no reason for living. We have no path to follow. To do what God created us to do, we must remain focused on God above all other things and submit to the leadership of the Holy Spirit for our direction. The Bible says in Lamentations 3:25, *"The Lord is good to those whose hope is in him, to the one who seeks him."*

Our second level of priorities should focus on what God wants us to do. Think about it this way: What has God given you a passion for? What gifts or talents has He given you to be used for God's glory? What weaknesses or life experiences has God nudged you with to keep you focused on Him? Maybe God wants you to do something big like run for public office or head up a corporation. Maybe He wants you to volunteer at a local school or hospital. Maybe He wants you to start a church in a foreign country. Whether your reason for living is big or small, in front of a large crowd or behind the scenes, worthy of fame and fortune, or something no one will ever know about, every mission from God is important and helps fulfill God's overall plan, your reason for living. Keeping your eyes focused on God, through the leadership of the Holy Spirit, is key to finding what God created you to do and staying connected to it. In Colossians 3:23-24 it says, *"Whatever you do, work at it with all your heart, as working for the Lord, not for human masters, since you know that you will receive an inheritance from the Lord as a reward. It is the Lord Christ you are serving."*

Our third and final level of priorities has to do with the people we surround ourselves with; the people we seek out and allow to be a part of our lives. Ask yourself, who are the people who mean the most to me and are important to my well-being and success? Who are the people who consistently lift my spirits and help me stay on track? Who are the pillars of my life, the people who give my life positive direction and meaning? These are the people we want around us. They are the people God has given us to support us on our journey.

Your ultimate goal with this priority is to identify all the people you want to have a major role in your life and make them a priority. They are the people who are important to your reason for living and will support you unconditionally in the good times and the bad. They are the people you want around you, no matter the cost, because they are good for you. Choose these people carefully. Keep them close. God has crossed your path with these people for a reason. The Bible says in Proverbs 12:26, *"The righteous choose their friends carefully, but the way of the wicked leads them astray."*

Experts tell us how we spend our time and money is a good indicator of what is important to us, what is a priority in our lives. Jesus agrees. In Matthew 6:21 He says, *"For where your treasure is, there your heart will be also."* One thing is for sure, if you don't focus on your priorities and allocate your resources to support them, they won't be priorities for long. Worst of all, you will lose focus on the thing or things God has created you to do and your life will remain empty, without meaning.

What's important to you? How are you spending your time and money? Are your resources focused on God? Are you listening to God for direction? Are you surrounding yourself with the people God has put in your life who are important to your success? The successful accomplishment of your reason for living depends on staying focused on these three priorities. Focus on your priorities and do what God created you to do! *"And we know that in all things God works for the good of those who love him, who have been called according to his purpose."* (Romans 8:28)

When we focus on our priorities, we simplify our lives. I'm not a math person, but this is simple math. When we focus on our priorities and eliminate the distractions which keep us from focusing on what God created us to do, we simplify our lives. Living this way doesn't necessarily make life any easier. Life will continue to happen and throw curve balls at us from time to time. However, when we stay focused on the things most important to accomplishing what God planned for our lives, our lives are much less complicated.

My Life Becomes Less Complicated

How does focusing on our priorities simplify our lives? The Bible says in Psalm 19:7 (MSG), *"The revelation of God is whole and pulls our lives together. The signposts of God are clear and point out the right road. The life-maps of God are right, showing the way to joy. The directions of God are plain and easy on the eyes. God's reputation is twenty-four-carat gold, with a lifetime guarantee. The decisions of God are accurate down to the nth degree."* When we stay focused on God's signposts, He will always show us the right road to follow. He shows us what's important and not so important. He shows us how to set our priorities and eliminate the things which get in the way of our reason for living. When we stay focused on the priorities God has established for our lives, we simplify the way we live our lives.

But more than just simplifying our lives, when we focus on God's plan for us, we replace the stress and complications in our lives with the satisfaction of a purpose, a God inspired purpose. There can be no greater drive in the world than accepting and accomplishing God's design for our lives. When we focus on what God created us to do, no longer do we worry about the little bumps in the road or the little sidebars of life because we know God is setting our path to follow. If He wants us to stop and smell the roses here and there from time to time, we know it's for a reason, a good reason. For example, maybe it is to help a person in need. Maybe it is to learn a valuable lesson we need to know that will nudge us back on the right path. Whatever our life's divergence is, it is given to us by God to prepare us for doing something He created us to do. Paul wrote in Ephesians 5:5-17, *"Be very careful, then, how you live—not as unwise but as wise, making the most of every opportunity, because the days are evil. Therefore do not be foolish, but understand what the Lord's will is."* Knowing and accepting this Godly truth simplifies our lives and helps us accept and tolerate life's little diversions when life happens.

How do we let our lives get so complicated in the first place? It's simple; we let our life's clutter – the noise in our lives – get in the way of our relationship with God. Because of our worldly self-centered focus, we take our eyes off God. And, without God's focus in our lives, fear drives our actions and we try to haphazardly find the path we think we should be on. We let things unrelated to our reason for living control our resources and complicate our lives.

Taking control of our time – our most valuable asset in the world – is essential to fulfilling our reason for living. To do this, we start by looking at how we spend our time. What are you spending your time doing? Are you productive with your time focusing on your life's purpose or are you just wasting your life away paying your bills until you die? Believe me brothers and sisters; this is no way to live!

I'm certain all of us feel as if we could use our time more efficiently doing what God created us to do. However God doesn't expect us to work 24/7. On the contrary, God knows we need time to rest and recharge our batteries. In Exodus 20:8-11 the Bible tells us, *"Remember the Sabbath day by keeping it holy. Six days you shall labor and do all your work, but the seventh day is a sabbath to the LORD your God. On it you shall not do any work, neither you, nor your son or daughter, nor your male or female servant, nor your animals, nor any foreigner residing in your towns. For in six days the LORD made the heavens and the earth, the sea, and all that is in them, but he rested on the seventh day. Therefore the LORD blessed the Sabbath day and made it holy."* Our downtime is so important to God He made it one of His Ten Commandments! If our day of rest is so important to God, don't you think it should just as important to us?

God doesn't expect us to do everything or be involved in every activity. God has a plan for our lives. He wants us to understand why he created us. He wants us to know what is and isn't important. He wants us to simplify our lives to a manageable level so we can focus on our real reason for living. Think about this: If we are focused on the wrong things – the clutter in our lives – how can we give enough time and attention to what God wants us to accomplish? Solomon in his old age wrote in Ecclesiastes 4:4 (ERV), *"Then I thought, "Why do people work so hard?" I saw people try to succeed and be better than other people. They do this because they are jealous. They don't want other people to have more than they have. This is senseless. It is like trying to catch the wind."*

I believe the clutter Solomon is talking about is broken down into three categories: relationships, commitments, and stuff. First, we have associations with people who are caustic to our relationship with God. These people try to tear us down and redirect our focus from God to other things. People who want to hurt us at every opportunity. As Jesus told his disciples, we must turn away from these people and shake the dust off our feet. (Mark 6:11) We must remove these people from our inner circle and let God deal with them directly.

The second type of clutter which distracts us from our reason for living is our commitments. Just as we sometimes let harmful relationships clutter our lives, we over commit ourselves to activities which prevent us from spending time on our more important priorities. This could be almost anything we can imagine. It could be a bowling league we've lost interest in. It could be a commitment to an organization taking more time than we were originally led to believe. It could be an extra project throwing us behind on more important work. Whatever it is, it is a commitment needlessly controlling our time. If possible, we must politely and gracefully eliminate anything falling into this category. In addition, in the future we must make sure whatever we are being asked to commit to is a priority in God's plan for our lives before we say yes. Anything we overcommit to which is not a God-driven priority steals our time with God and the relationship He wants to have with us.

The final type of clutter is our stuff. Having more stuff than we really need clutters our lives and directly affects our ability to do what God created us to do. How does this happen? We develop an "I may need this someday" mindset or think

"This might be worth something someday." What happens when we do this? We never get rid of it! Our stuff builds up around us and it takes over our space, our lives, and occupies our time taking care of it. Anything not helping us focus on our priorities is a hindrance to our life's purpose and what God created us to accomplish.

Sadly, the average American only has 79 years to live and accomplish their God-given purpose.[2] God expects us to use our time wisely in this pursuit. God purposely gave us a path to follow in order for us to learn and grow into the people He wants us to become. How we use our time focusing on God and the priorities He has given us will determine how successful we are in accomplishing our reason for living. Do we want to squander our time away on activities unrelated to our God-given purpose and waste our lives – or – do we want to focus on God, let Him show us our path to follow, and simplify our lives of the things which get in the way of us doing what God created us to do? The Living Bible tells us in Hebrews 12:1, *"Let us strip off anything that slows us down or holds us back ... and let us run with patience the particular race that God has set before us."*

When we focus on the priorities God has given us and eliminate the distractions that get in the way of us focusing on God's plan for our lives, our success is assured.

My Success Is Assured

Think about this: How successful do you think the Alabama Crimson Tide Football Team would be if they ignored the instructions of their coaches? Alabama, with 16 national and 25 Southeastern Conference titles, is unquestionably one of the most successful college football programs in the history of the game. But tell me, how successful do you think Alabama would be if the players ignored their coaches?

Every play in a football game is a microcosm of life with game changing implications. Before every snap of the ball, each player evaluates the situation they face to determine their role based on their coaches' instructions. Once the ball is snapped, using their gifts, abilities, and past experience, each player executes their assignment in coordination with their teammates to position their team for the win. Once the play has ended, each player picks himself up off the ground, celebrates his accomplishments, learns from his mistakes, and quickly prepares for the next play. Sometimes the play results in a touchdown, however most of the time the play only moves the line of scrimmage a few yards. Whatever happens, every play is important to the final outcome of the contest and requires every player's full attention to what they know, what they have been taught, and what they have been assigned to do. Football – like life – is a game of what have's, should have's, and could have's which ultimately determines the result of the game and the successes they all share.

Now, think what would happen if none of the players at Alabama paid attention to their coaches, prepared for the game, or took their assignments seriously? Do you think they would be as successful as they are today? Of course not! Instead of being known as one of the greatest programs in college football history, most people – except for a few die-hard Alabama fans – wouldn't know anything about them. Alabama would never be on TV. They would never play in big games. They would be forgotten in history.

Why is Alabama so successful? The answer is obvious. When each player seriously prepares for the game and uses their gifts and abilities to execute the assignments given to them by their coaches, nothing can stop them. They are successful because everyone is committed to the program's standards. They are committed to the coaches, their assignment, and to each other. And when everyone buys in and is totally committed to the goals of the team, their success is assured. In fact, the individual players are not just successful, the team, the coaches, and everyone else associated with the program is successful too.

Life is no different from football. When we actively talk to God, listen to His instructions, and complete our assignments using the tools He has given us, our success is also assured. But not only is our success assured, the people God puts along our path are successful too. Just as a football player is asked to put the needs of the team before their own, we are commanded to love our neighbors as ourselves and put their needs before ours. When we're plugged into God's plan for our lives and use the tools God has given us to be successful accomplishing our reason for living, we help the people God puts along our path become successful too, and our success – God's success – is multiplied even more.

In Luke 6:38 (ERV) the Bible says, *"Give to others, and you will receive. You will be given much. It will be poured into your hands—more than you can hold. You will be given so much that it will spill into your lap. The way you give to others is the way God will give to you."*

However, to be as successful as God wants us to be, we must trust Him completely. Like the Alabama football players must totally trust their coaches to reach their full potential as an individual and as a team, we must trust God unconditionally. The Bible says in Proverbs 3:5-6 (ICB), *"Trust the Lord with all your heart. Don't depend on your own understanding. Remember the Lord in everything you do. And he will give you success."* God wants us to be winners in the game of life. And when we are successful doing what He created us to do, God's people are successful too, and His plan is advanced in the world.

God created and designed each of us with a reason for living. He gave us tools to aid us in our pursuit of our God-given purpose. He teaches us about His love and how we are to love others. He gives us opportunities and assignments. He guides us in every situation so we may be successful. He picks us up when we fall down and forgives us when we fail. He imparts wisdom to us when we least expect it, in the good times and in the bad. He multiplies our successes when we completely trust Him and follow His direction. As long as we keep our eyes focused on God – our life coach – He will ensure our success and the successes of those we are sent to love. *"And God is able to bless you abundantly, so that in all things at all times, having all that you need, you will abound {flourish} in every good work."* (2 Corinthians 9:8) When we focus on God and completely trust Him with our lives, our success is assured as we fulfill God's plan – our reason for living – in the world.

By this point in the book, I'm sure you have realized if you're not happy with the path your life is taking, you're looking for happiness in all the wrong places. Sustaining happiness comes through understanding your God-given purpose, accepting and owning the gifts and tools you have been given by God, focusing on your God-given priorities and supporting them with your resources, sharing yourself with others in love, and getting rid of everything else not supporting your reason for living. This is God's process for finding sustaining happiness or joy. Jesus said in Matthew 6:33 (CEV), *"But more than anything else, put God's work first and do what he wants. Then the other things will be yours as well."* Your joy will come naturally.

My Sustaining Happiness, My Joy Comes Naturally

Not including God in our decision making process is where most people mess up. When making life decisions – choices which have a direct effect on our happiness – we exclude God. Who we marry, where we work, who we pick as friends, where we live, where we go to church, are just a few of the life decisions we all have to make which will ultimately determine how happy we become. For example, if we pick the wrong person to marry, the relationship will be turbulent at best and could possibly end in divorce. If we pick the wrong job, we will never be fully committed to the goals of the company or perform our best work. If we pick the wrong friends to spend our time with, we will most likely be labeled as someone we're not and may be persuaded to let our lives go in directions we are not prepared to go. If we pick the wrong place to live, we may be separated from our family – our built-in support system – and become isolated from everyone we love and who loves us. If we pick the wrong church, we may never assimilate into the family of God or experience the love from fellow believers as God intended. Let's face it. There is nothing happy about a bad marriage, an unfulfilling job, the wrong friends, an unhappy living arrangement, or a church where you sit in a pew and don't know anyone.

The good news: God didn't design the world this way. He wants His children to be happy. The Bible says in Ecclesiastes 3:12-13, *"I know that there is nothing better for people than to be happy and to do good while they live. That each of them may eat and drink, and find satisfaction in all their toil—this is the gift of God."* And because happiness is a gift from God, no matter how hard we may try, we cannot be truly happy without God in our lives.

God created each of us in our mother's womb to be happy. And when we love our neighbors with all the tools God has given us to support our reason for living, we are happy. This happiness is not a feeling which only fills our hearts momentarily. Our happiness is a sustaining joy which lasts for eternity. It comes to us naturally as it was designed and promised to us by God!

My wife and I met in the fourth grade at Highland Park Elementary School. We sat across the aisle from each other in Ms. Sheldon's class. Little did either of us know at the time we would end up getting married some 11 years later.

As a 10-year-old boy, you don't think about marriage. In fact, at the time, I didn't even like girls that much. I was into sports – football, baseball, basketball – and really didn't have time for girls.

However, sitting across the aisle from someone for an entire year makes them impossible to ignore. We talked. We did assignments together. And we may have even hung out on the playground a few times during year. But believe me when I tell you this: I didn't want a girlfriend, nor did I want a friend who was a girl.

The next year Mary went to a different school in the system and I didn't see her again until the sixth grade. Although we didn't have many classes together throughout our middle and high school years, we became friends and talked whenever we could. You see, Mary is a lot smarter than me and she was assigned to much more advanced classes. I was a jock. I wanted to spend my spare time playing sports, not studying nor doing homework.

In the summer before our junior year, Mary and I spent some quality time with each other at church camp, studying God's word. In late summer each year, as I mentioned before, several of the local Baptist churches in the area pooled their resources and took their youth for Bible study and fellowship for a week in the mountains of Tennessee at Camp NaCoMe. I was on a break from fall football practice and she was on break from marching band camp. It was a great week with a lot of people making decisions for the Lord. It was especially good for me. For reasons unknown to me at the time, God helped me make a real connection with Mary and we started dating. For the next six years we were inseparable. She not only became my girlfriend, she became my best friend.

With God's help we tried to do everything the right way within our relationship. We remained virgins until our wedding night. We studied the scripture and doctorial statements of various denominations before deciding where we would go to church. We secured good jobs and built a sufficient savings account to put us on solid financial ground before our wedding date. We did everything we could think of to build a relationship which would last for eternity. I'm proud to tell you all the work we put into our relationship while we were dating paid off. Mary and I have been married for over 38 years. She is still my best friend.

Like all couples, we've had good and bad times. We've made mistakes along the way. We've been in unfulfilling jobs. We've made parenting mistakes. We've made decisions not in the best interest of our family. But thanks to God, we've had some great successes too. I wish I had more time to tell you about how God has worked in our lives throughout the years to lead us to where we are today. Maybe I'll write a book someday. (smile)

In hindsight, Mary and I can clearly see how God put us in situations to help us grow and mature. We can see where He moved us from town to town and from job to job to give us experiences we would need later in life. Personally, I have never been happier than I am now and it is a direct result of letting God – reluctantly at times – steer the wheel of my boat and direct my life's path.

God wants His children to be happy. Don't be fooled by those who try to tell you God is only in our lives to punish us when we do something wrong. This is a bold face lie! The Bible says in

Ecclesiastes 2:24-26, *"A person can do nothing better than to eat and drink and find satisfaction in their own toil. This too, I see, is from the hand of God, for without him, who can eat or find enjoyment? To the person who pleases him, God gives wisdom, knowledge and happiness."* God wants us to be happy. He wants us to be filled with His joy. He wants us to take the joy and love He gives us and share it with the world. But the happiness you're seeking —the emptiness you're trying to fill – can't be attained without God's involvement in every detail of your life. Sustaining happiness is the result of a natural process God created. And it only comes from God.

When we love God and love God's people as He loves us, real joy – sustaining joy – happens! As God designed it, we are to love those around us, wherever we are. We are to love people at work, in our neighborhood, at the local grocery store, or anywhere we come in contact with people in our community. You see, when we trust God completely and love His people as He created us to love, happiness follows naturally and we fulfill God's plan – our God-given purpose – and do what God created us to do. Best of all, we build up treasures, not on earth, but in heaven.

My Treasures Are Stored In Heaven

We live in a world which promotes "more is better." We have falsely been led to believe we can never have enough of anything. For example, if we had more money, all our problems would go away. If we had more time, we could get more done. If we had more education or education from a more prestigious school, we could have a rewarding career dreams are made from. This is a lie too!

Think about this: We don't really own anything in this life. We're born into this world with nothing, and when the time comes, we leave this place the same way — with nothing. We only borrow the things we have in this life for a short while and then give them to someone else when we die. In time, this person gives our things — their things — to someone else. Having all the money, time, and quality education in the universe will not stop this inevitable process from running its course.

So, based on the realities of life, if we can't take anything with us to heaven when we die, why do we put so much importance on the things of this world while we are living? Why do we have this "more is better" mentality? It's because the world's influence causes us to focus on the wrong things. Instead of focusing on how much more money, time, or education we can acquire, we should be thankful for what has been given to us – loaned to us – and focus more on how it should be used.

Everything we have in this world is a gift from God. Without God we would not exist. We would not have a place to live. There would be no money to spend. There would be no time to squander. There would be no schools to prepare us for our careers. Everything we are, everything we have, and everything we have the potential to become in this world and in life is the direct result of God's love for us. Without God, our universe, our world, our very existence would not be possible.

But God didn't end His design with the formation of the universe and everything in it. From the beginning, God never intended for our lives to end at death. In addition to the planet we live on, God created a place where those who lovingly follow Him could be with Him for eternity. God calls this place heaven.

Heaven is a place like no other. It's one of a kind. The Bible tells us the walls around heaven are made from every kind of precious stone. The city and its streets are made of gold so pure it looks like transparent glass. The gates into the city are made out of a single pearl. Heaven is a place where every believer will live together. It's a place where loved ones will be reunited. It's a place where we will be rewarded for our good service and how we loved our neighbors. Heaven is a place where we will be given assignments based on our God-given gifts and how we developed and matured them on Earth. It's a place where God's people will no longer suffer with earthly things. We will no longer be troubled with sin, suffering, sickness, sadness, or death. In heaven, these things no longer exist. Heaven is a place – likened to a wedding banquet – where we will eat, drink, and celebrate with God and each other for eternity.

However, the only way you can live in heaven is to accept Jesus Christ as your Lord and Savior and follow Him. There is no other way. You can't buy your way in. You can't talk your way in. You can't ever be good enough to get in. The only way you live in heaven is by asking for forgiveness of your sins, believing in God, and accepting His gift of eternal life.

The moment you accept Jesus Christ and put Him in control of your life, your real life begins. With the Holy Spirit in control, it's no longer important for you to build riches on Earth. It's no longer important to collect things which can't be taken with you into heaven. It's no longer important to be better than someone else. If your heart is focused on the right things, your attention changes from earthly possessions to loving God's people and preparing your place in heaven.

Unfortunately, not everyone chooses Jesus Christ as their Savior. They purposely shun Him and block Him from their lives. They turn their back on Him and say they don't need a savior. They curse His name and the people who follow Him. God has a place for these people too. It's called hell. And it is the exact opposite of heaven. The Bible tells us it's a fiery lake of burning sulfur where the fire never goes out. A place filled with pain. It's a place where people are punished for eternity. Most significantly, it is a place where people are separated from God forever. Why would anyone choose to spend eternity there?

When it comes down to it, the choice is ours. Either we choose to be with God for eternity or we throw ourselves into the fiery lake of burning sulfur when we die. God is not going to interfere with our decision. He purposely – by design – gave us the right to choose where we spend eternity.

Just like God will not interfere with the biggest decision of our lives, no one can make this decision for us. Either we live for God or we isolate ourselves from Him. Either we love God and His people as He designed it or we sentence ourselves to live in a place void of love forever. Please choose wisely!

Only when we focus on God and use our resources to complete our God-given purpose – the reason for our entire existence – do we become the people we were created to be on Earth and develop into the persons we were born to become in heaven. Only then can we prepare treasures in heaven we will enjoy for eternity.

What did God create you to do? Why are you here? I pray you will prayerfully open up a dialogue with God and search out His direction. Until you do, you will never know.

If you still need to accept Jesus Christ as your Savior and follow Him, please go to the Appendix How To Become A Child Of God for instructions on how to receive God's grace.

Endnotes

[1] *Encarta World English Dictionary*, Online Version, s.v. "copy-edit."

[2] Central Intelligence Agency (CIA), "The World Factbook," cia.gov, USA.gov, https://www.cia.gov/library/publications/the-world-factbook/rankorder/2102rank.html

My Hope For You

Throughout this book we have looked at several questions concerning what God created us to do, our reason for living. These simple questions were designed to help you find your God-given purpose and do the work which will bring you the sustaining joy you are seeking.

For some of us, it may have been life changing. We found our place in the world and learned how we are to use the tools God has given us. We understand God's plan for the world and our role in it. We know how to look for and find sustaining happiness. Our priorities began to focus. Our lives became less complicated as we started living our lives as God intended.

Others of us just went through the motions. Our heart wasn't in the right place, we didn't take the book seriously, and we gleaned little from it. For those of you who fall into this category, I am truly sorry. I'm sorry I let you down. I'm sorry I let God down. I pray you will block out time in your busy schedule and go back through the book again and prayerfully listen to God as He shows you, through His word, what He has in store for your life. If you listen closely and let the Holy Spirit lead you, I promise your life will never be the same. You will know specifically why you are here and what you are to do with your life. The life God intended for you to live – your real life – will begin!

Isn't that what we all want? Don't we all want to understand our real purpose, our reason for living? Without God in our lives, it is impossible to know why we are here. After all, God is the creator of the universe. He created every living thing in it, each with a purpose to support the others. The only way we can really know what God created us to do is by talking to God, the One who assigned to us our reason for living. Without God in our lives, we are just feeling our way around in the darkness with no clue where to look for answers.

I think our reason for living can be summarized in four verses in the Bible. You probably saw them listed in the first few pages of this book. These four verses embody God's plan for us and our purpose in the world.

For God so loved the world that he gave his one and only Son, that whoever believes in him shall not perish but have eternal life. (John 3:16)

From the beginning, God loved us unconditionally. He wanted us to live with Him for eternity. In fact, He loved us so much He was willing to let His son die on a cross for our sins. This unselfish act wiped our sins away and gives us access to heaven where God lives.

But only we can choose to go to heaven. God made it possible through the death of Jesus and His resurrection when He ascended into heaven to live with His father, God. It was God's intention from the beginning for us to follow Jesus at our deaths into heaven to be with Him. He only gave us one requirement. We accept Jesus Christ as our Lord and Savior.

Love the Lord your God with all your heart and with all your soul and with all your mind and with all your strength. **(Mark 12:30; Matthew 22:37)**

Like God loves us, we are to love Him completely, with our entire being. What do I mean by loving Him with our entire being? I think the love God expects from us is best illustrated in Genesis 22: 1-19 when God tested Abraham's love by asking him to sacrifice his son Isaac. On God's direction, Abraham took his son to a mountain in the region of Moriah three days away. With Isaac bound tightly on an altar of wood, Abraham raised his knife high above Isaac ready to slay his son. Just as Abraham's knife started to plunge into Isaac's body, the angel of the Lord called out to Abraham and stopped him. *"Do not lay a hand on the boy,"* he said. *"Do not do anything to him. Now I know that you fear God, because you have not withheld from me your son, your only son."* (Genesis 22:12) Loving God with our entire being is shown by demonstrating to God we are willing – without question – to sacrifice something of great importance to us. Like God's love for us when He allowed His only son to be sacrificed for us, we must be willing to sacrifice everything we love in this world for Him.

But not only are we to love God with all our being, we are to love our neighbor the same way.

Love your neighbor as yourself. (Mark 12:31; Matthew 22:39)

We are to love our neighbors as ourselves. It's The Golden Rule in action. Jesus said in Matthew 7:12 (Phillips), *"Treat other people exactly as you would like to be treated by them."* By anyone's standard, these are wise words to live by. In fact, if everyone in the world lived by this one rule, we could eliminate all the evil in the world.

Unfortunately, the devil gets in our way. We allow him to convince us we are better than others. We allow him to sway us into believing we deserve more privileges or rights than other people. The devil causes us to feel like we are more special than everyone around us, and we deserve to be treated differently. If we are not careful, it becomes our driving force and we turn our eyes away from God, and our neighbors we are commanded by God to love, are forgotten. As a result, today most of us don't even know who our next-door neighbors are, nor do we want to know. *Lord, please forgive us.*

The Golden Rule is a simple concept. If we want people to respect us, we must first respect them. If we want people to value us, we must first value them. If we want people to love us, we must first love them. In essence, we must model to others how we want to be treated.

But not only are we to love our neighbors as ourselves, we must be willing to die for them. This is how God measures our love for our neighbors. The Bible says in 1 John 3:16, *"This is how we know what love is: Jesus Christ laid down his life for us. And we ought to lay down our lives for our brothers and sisters."* If we don't love our neighbor enough to be willing to die for them, we don't really love our neighbors as God commanded us to love them.

I think it is interesting John 3:16 and 1 John 3:16 give us direction about how we are to love. By letting His son die for us on a cross, God demonstrated to us how much He loves us. In the same way, we are to show how much we love our neighbors by being willing to die for them. To really love God with all our heart, soul, mind, and strength we must be willing to lay down our lives for God and our neighbors. Our love for God and our neighbors has no limitations.

The best way to love God and our neighbors is by using the tools God has given us to love. Our passions, likes and dislikes, gifts, talents, and skills were given to us by God to fulfill His plan, our reason for living. In addition, God gives us life experiences and points out our weaknesses from time to time in order to help us grow and keep us on track to accomplish His plan for our lives. When you reduce our reason for living down to the smallest common denominator, we are here to love God and our neighbors unconditionally with the tools He has created within us to accomplish our assigned tasks.

To do this we are commanded to leave our comfort zone and love people everywhere.

All authority in heaven and on earth has been given to me. Therefore go and make disciples of all nations, baptizing them in the name of the Father and of the Son and of the Holy Spirit, and teaching them to obey everything I have commanded you. And surely I am with you always, to the very end of the age. (Matthew 28:18-20)

To do what God created us to do, we are to make disciples of every nation loving them as God loves us. For some of us, this means leaving our families and moving to remote regions of the world. For most of us, however, it means loving people right where we live. My church calls it "Love Where You Are."[1] We are to love people like God loves us wherever we are – in our neighborhood, community, church, work, or anywhere God takes us. The location where we love people is not as important as how we show our love for those we come in contact with wherever we are. Loving God and loving our neighbors as God commanded us to love them is what's important.

There you have it! Our reason for living summarized in four Bible verses. I pray you find your God-given purpose and do what God created you to do! Your sustaining happiness, your sustaining joy in this world depends on it. May God bless you and your family as you seek God's plan – your God-given purpose – for your life and do what God created you to do!

Endnotes

[1] Dave Stone, "Love Where You Are," southeastchristian.org, Southeast Christian Church, Louisville, KY, https://www.southeastchristian.org/sermons/love-where-you-are/

Appendix – How To Become A Child Of God

I'm so happy you have decided to follow Jesus! You are not here at this crossroad by chance. God loves you and has a reason for your life.

From the moment you were conceived in your mother's womb, God had a plan for you and gave you the passions, likes and dislikes, gifts and talents, and a family to give you direction about who you are to become. As part of the maturing process, God gave you life experiences which led you to this point in your life and will continue to shape and prepare you for the great works God has in store for you. If you have never confessed Jesus Christ as your Lord and Savior, this is the first step to living your life intentionally and doing what God created you to do.

167

The following Bible passages explain how to become a child of God. Most call this sequence of verses the Romans Road to Salvation. Follow it closely. Sincerely pray the Prayer of Salvation and allow the Holy Spirit into your heart and take hold of the love of God. He is waiting for you!

Romans Road To Salvation

"For all have sinned and fall short of the glory of God." (Romans 3:23)

We have all sinned. We have all done things not pleasing to God. None of us can ever be good enough to get into heaven. We need God's help to live forever.

"For the wages of sin is death, but the gift of God is eternal life in Christ Jesus our Lord." (Romans 6:23)

The consequence of sin is death, an eternity separated from God. We can't buy our way into heaven. We can't talk our way into heaven. The only way we can get into heaven is through Jesus

Christ. Because of God's grace – His willingness to forgive us of our sin – we are saved from death.

"But God demonstrates his own love for us in this: While we were still sinners, Christ died for us." (Romans 5:8)

God freely offered His only son Jesus Christ so He could die on a cross for our sins. With Jesus' death, He paid the penalty for our sins once and for all. Our sins are paid in full.

"If you declare with your mouth, "Jesus is Lord," and believe in your heart that God raised him from the dead, you will be saved. For it is with your heart that you believe and are justified, and it is with your mouth that you profess your faith and are saved." (Romans 10:9-10)

To be saved from death, all we have to do is believe in our heart Jesus was raised from the dead and confess with our mouth Jesus is Lord. The act of God raising Jesus from the dead made it possible for all of us to overcome death. With our confession, we are saved from death and are promised eternal life with God in heaven when we die. Romans 10:13 says, *"Everyone who calls on the name of the Lord will be saved."*

> *"**For God so loved the world that he gave his one and only Son, that whoever believes in him shall not perish but have eternal life.**"* (John 3:16)

God loved us so much, He freely allowed His son Jesus to be sacrificed, saving us from our sin. So if we believe in Him, we can live with Him forever in heaven.

Are you ready to accept the gift of eternal life from God? Bow your head and sincerely pray the following prayer.

Prayer Of Salvation

Father, I know I am a sinner. I know I deserve punishment. Thank you for letting Jesus take the punishment for me with His death on the cross. I believe with all my heart and soul you raised Jesus from the dead, paying the full penalty for my sins.

I know I need a Savior and I freely confess Jesus is Lord and Savior of all and surrender control of my life to Him. I know He has a plan for my life and I want to fulfill His will in the world and do what God created me to do. I place my trust in you and seek your leadership in all things. Thank you for your grace and the gift of eternal life. Amen!

***

Welcome to the family of God! Asking Jesus to come into your heart and be your Lord and Savior is the first step in understanding your reason for living and doing what God created you to do. As soon as you can, please follow Him through baptism, plug yourself into a local church community, and actively serve your brothers and sisters in Christ and let them serve you as we all prepare for our missions in the world. I thank God for you and wish you all the best!

May God richly bless you and direct your work as you do what God created you to do!

The Author

Bobby G. Muse, Jr is passionate about helping people do what God created them to do. When we submit to our Lord and Savior's leadership and use the unique gifts, passions, and abilities He so graciously gives us, we find our reason for living and experience the real joy God intended for us.

Bobby is married to his high school sweetheart, Mary. They met while sitting across the aisle from each other in the fourth grade. Bobby and Mary have been happily married for over 38 years and have two wonderful children, Jonathan and Kristen.

In his free time, Bobby follows Alabama football, goes to Disney World whenever he can, and volunteers backstage in the Worship Tech Ministry at Southeast Christian Church in Louisville, Kentucky.

CONNECT
WITH BOBBY!

BobbyGMuse

@BobbyGMuse

BobbyGMuse.com